Pie in the Sky

the Authorized History of Punkin Chunkin'

Also by Bob Kotowski, published by Cedar Tree Books Ltd.:

Ablaze in Lewes Harbor:
the Last Cruise of the SS Lenape

Pie in the Sky

the Authorized History of Punkin Chunkin'

BOB KOTOWSKI

WILMINGTON, DELAWARE

Pie in the Sky: the Authorized History of Punkin Chunkin'

First Printing, 2008

Published by: Cedar Tree Books Ltd.
             P.O. Box 4256
             Wilmington, DE 19807
             books@ctpress.com
             www.cedartreebooks.com

ISBN 10: 1-892142-40-6
ISBN 13: 978-1-892142-40-5

Title: Pie in the Sky: the Authorized History of Punkin Chunkin'
Author: Bob Kotowski
Editor: Nicholas L. Cerchio III
Book Design and Layout: Bob Schwartz

Library of Congress Cataloging-in-Publication Data

Kotowski, Bob.
Pie in the sky : the authorized history of punkin chunkin' / by Bob Kotowski.
    p. cm.
Includes bibliographical references.
ISBN-13: 978-1-892142-40-5 (alk. paper)
ISBN-10: 1-892142-40-6 (alk. paper)
1. Sussex County (Del.)--Social life and customs. 2. Pumpkin--Competitions--Delaware--Sussex County--History. 3.
Contests--Delaware--Sussex County--History. 4. Sussex County (Del.)--Biography. I. Title.

F172.S8K68 2008
790.1'5--dc22

2008035390

Printed and bound in the United States of America

DEDICATION

Pie in the Sky: the Authorized History of Punkin Chunkin' is dedicated to the three teams who chunked the first "punkins" in Sussex County, Delaware, and started it all—John Ellsworth and Donald "Doc" Pepper, William "Broad Dog" Thompson and the late William "Trey" Melson, and the "notorious" brothers Chuck and Darryl Burton—and to all the chunkers who came after them, especially the as-yet-unknown punkin chunker who hurls a gourd a mile.

PREFACE

If **Punkin Chunkin'** were in the dictionary, the entry probably would be something like this:

> **Pun-kin Chun-kin** \'pən-kən 'chən-kən\ *n. often attrib* [alter. of *pumpi-on*, F. *pompon*, L. *pepon*, Gk *pepō*]; var. of *pumpkin chucking*. **1:** the art and science of tossing or hurling a round, deep yellow gourd of the family *Cucurbita pepo* through the use of a modified version of an ancient siege machine or variant of a piece of military artillery. **2:** a contest among teams to see whose pumpkin travels farthest intact, with the World Championship held annually the first weekend of November in Sussex County, Delaware. **3:** founded as a personal challenge in Slower Lower Delaware in 1986 and attributed to four men referred to by *Cape Gazette* Sports Editor Dave Frederick as "Renaissance Rednecks." **4:** homegrown insanity. **5:** organized insanity. **6:** organized chaos. **7:** a fine madness. **8:** the biggest tailgate party in Southern Delaware.

Punkin chunkin' may not be in any standard lexicon, but it is in the vocabulary of more than a hundred teams who vie for small class trophies, bragging rights and, for the World Record Team, possession—if only for a year—of a gnarly life-sized wooden trophy very loosely modeled on the marble statue of the Greek Titan Atlas in the *Museo Archeologico Nazionale* in Naples, Italy.

Punkin chunkin' also is in the vocabulary of tens of thousands of spectators who travel from other states and other countries each year to a field in Sussex County, Delaware, and get caught up in the mayhem that has grown from a friendly challenge among a handful of men to a major tourist attraction in the state.

Over the years, the World Championship Punkin Chunkin' Association also has grown into a major charitable organization, raising and distributing tens of thousands of dollars a year to various charities and to individual scholarships.

Chunkin', or "chucking" as linguistic purists would say, has expanded to contests in nearly every state, Canada and Europe. One of the more powerful machines, an air cannon from Illinois, is in the <u>Guinness Book of World Records</u> for chunking a pumpkin 4491 feet. As far as the chunkers are concerned, though, the only record that counts is the one set at the annual Delaware event: a launch of just over 4434 feet by an air cannon from Michigan.

World Championship Punkin Chunkin' trophy.
Photo by Delaware Digital Video Factory, official videographer
of the World Championship Punkin Chunkin' since 1999.
Reprinted with permission.

In more than two decades of what amounts to tossing fruit great distances, media from all over the world—newspapers, magazines, radio stations, television networks and documentary channels—have featured punkin chunkin' in hundreds, if not thousands, of reports. Research for this book relies heavily on many of those media stories. It also, where possible, relies on records from the World Championship Punkin Chunkin' Association. But, in a group that grew out of a competition among friends and has gone through several changes, record keeping has sometimes taken a backseat over the years to efforts to build the perfect hurling engine. So, gaps have had to be filled with anecdotal information, an imperfect source that often becomes colored by time, memory and perception.

This book is not intended to be a compilation or pictorial of every team that has ever chunked a pumpkin. It is a history of how the competition started and how it has changed since 1986, with emphasis on significant events in punkin chunkin's development.

FOREWORD

As a child, like every other child, I had the desire to throw things. From food to rocks to baseballs I threw them all. I guess that would explain my addiction and even passion for the sport of punkin chunkin'.

In 1992, I was assigned to the chunk as a paramedic working in the firing pits and knew almost immediately I wanted to be part of the event. John Ellsworth was kind enough to allow me on his team and my life has never been the same since. From the first trip to New York City to be on the David Letterman Show to the most current chunk, my addiction has grown and grown. I have not missed a day of chunkin' since.

The legend of punkin chunkin' has been told many times with as many variations but the fact remains that there is no greater joy than meeting old and new friends on the field of play the first weekend in November to throw pumpkins. Whether you are a first-time chunker or one of the founders, you are part of a huge caring family for those three days.

Talk to any of the spectators and they will say one of two things: 1) 95% say they are addicted for life; 2) the other 5% think they passed some outlet stores on the way in and are going to look for them. From business people to scout troops, they want to be a part of chunkin'. Doctors, lawyers, plumbers, sales people, and any other profession imaginable are represented on the firing line and in the spectator area during the World Championship Punkin Chunkin' weekend in Sussex County, Delaware. The very young to the very experienced in life come to compete or watch. They come from all walks of life and enjoy the chunk.

There is something for everyone at the chunk. In addition to the three days of chunkin', there are over 150 vendors of all kinds, live entertainment on stage, rides, fireworks and even big name country entertainers on stage.

All this and chunkin' too. If you have not experienced the chunk it is time. If you have then I know I will be seeing you there on the first weekend in November.

Frank E. Shade
President
World Championship
Punkin Chunkin' Association

TABLE OF CONTENTS

ACKNOWLEDGEMENTS

Grateful appreciation to Cedar Tree Books publisher Nick Cerchio for suggesting the topic; to my wife Paula for her support, encouragement and patient proofreading; to Bob Schwartz at Fotografics for awesome layout and design; to World Championship Punkin Chunkin' Association President Frank Shade and to the association itself for opening their files and records to me; to Don Pepper, John Ellsworth and Bill Thompson for providing details of chunkin' in the beginning; to Betty Melson, Terry Brewster, Trish Nelson and Eric Nelson for sharing memories of Trey Melson; to Chuck Burton for sharing memories of chunks from day one to now; to Jake Burton for providing information on what it's like to be the next generation; to Capt. "Speed" Lackhove for letting everyone know they're never too old to have fun; to chunker and first president Larry McLaughlin for sharing his thoughts, memories and perspective and for providing documentation of the early years and details of the early organization; to Bill Sharp for giving his perspective on being a local member of an out-of state team; to Mike Hazzard for providing details of the first air cannon; to Diane Zigman, Margie Brenneman and Stephanie Coulbourne for the women's perspective; to Lana Browne for her story about a close encounter with a punkin chunker; to Tina Thoroughgood for providing early photographs; to Jim Riley of "Team PumpkinHammer," Steve Seigars of "Yankee Siege" and Ray Buchta at Delaware Digital Video Factory for several later pictures, and to Thompson, Ellsworth and Pepper for reading the final draft for accuracy and suggesting changes.

Pie in the Sky

the Authorized History of Punkin Chunkin'

MAMA SAID, "WE DON'T THROW THINGS"

The only way to understand why grown men and women would spend a lot of time and money to launch pumpkins down a field is to accept that it's perfectly natural. Mothers through the ages have been telling their offspring, "We don't throw things," only to find out that their progeny continue to do so. Frank Shade, president of the World Championship Punkin Chunkin' Association, said all you have to do is watch an infant or a toddler. Give a child a rattle or other toy and he or she will throw it on the floor to watch Mom pick it up. Put some food on a toddler's highchair tray and he or she will throw it to either indicate he or she is done, to show that it's distasteful or just to watch it splat on the floor.

People just throw things, like nearly every human who's walked the earth before them. Even chimpanzees, the nearest relative to early man on the evolutionary chain, throw things. They've been observed throwing sticks, rocks, dirt, feces, leaves and bits of food at predators and other chimpanzees in an effort to chase them away. Early humans, bipedal and possessing an opposable thumb as well, just naturally continued the act, usually throwing rocks and sticks in an effort to drive away predators or to hunt small game. They, and those who came after, not only threw things as a warning or to hunt, they sometimes threw out of frustration or anger. They sometimes threw in war, sometimes to compete and sometimes just because they could.

Anyone who's studied history at all or watched news coverage of more current events unfold knows that people often will pick up something to heave in protest of something they don't like. Bricks may sometimes be thrown at windows or police or soldiers or anything that stands in the way of their beliefs. But, historically, one of the favorite items to throw in protest is rotten food. It's messy and really gets the point across. One of the earlier records of tossing food involves the Roman Vespasian in the 1st century CE. Before he became Emperor, Vespasian was a general and a politician, but not all of his policies were popular. To show their displeasure, some of the common folk pelted him on the street with rotten turnips.

Politicians weren't the only ones subjected to being hit with something that had been or should have been in the stew pot. Ancient Greek theatergoers often would show boredom by throwing small stones and pieces of food at actors. Audiences in Elizabethan England rewarded actors they liked by tossing coins onto the stage. In the same respect, they rewarded bad acting by tossing rotten food at the stage. It's a practice that seemed to suit at least a couple of audiences in New York a few hundred years later. John Ritchie made his stage debut on Long Island in 1883 but was driven off by an onslaught of rotten tomatoes and eggs, never to return to that theater. Five years later, Dr. S. M. Landis met a similar fate in the Big Apple, but solved his problem by appearing the next night behind a large net stretched across the stage.

In the 18th century and earlier, people put in the pillories and condemned prisoners being taken to the executioner often were pelted with everything from rotten eggs and vegetables to dead cats.

But it's students in school cafeterias who have done the real food throwing, probably a throwback to their toddler years. Cafeteria food fights, best exemplified by the scene in the movie "Animal House," bring in at least two of the basic reasons to throw things: protesting the quality of the food and just sheer fun. Of course, there's also the "egging" that goes on around the country on Mischief Night.

For pure messy pleasure, though, the townsfolk of Buñol, Spain, have held a tomato festival—La Tomatina—since 1945 that culminates in a massive tomato fight attended by up to 30,000 people. Townsfolk and vistiors to the annual pre-Lenten carnival in Ivrea, a northwestern Italy town, engage in a furious battle to

reenact a medieval peasant revolt by vigorously pitching oranges at one another. Like punkin chunkers, they proudly have teams involved in throwing the fruit. But punkin chunkers throw for distance, not at one another.

Though throwing food may be fun, seeing who could throw just about anything the farthest has long just been part of the competitive nature of humans. It isn't known who was the first to "chunk" something as sport, but the two most cited cultures for competitive tossing are Greece and Scotland.

The Greek Games, which evolved into the modern Olympics, were recorded as early as 776 BCE, though there's evidence to suggest that they'd been going on since as far back as the 13th century BCE. Though the first known games were foot races, throwing later became part of the competition: the discus, the javelin and, ultimately, the shot put. Early Egyptians also held spear-throwing (javelin) competitions.

The Scots started the Highland Games in the 11th century CE. Like the Greeks, they began with foot races. But there also always has been an element of strength involved, usually by seeing who could throw something the farthest: the caber toss, hammer throw, stone put, weight throw, sheaf toss and the stone over the bar.

Over the centuries, throwing competitions have evolved—if "evolved" is the right word—and have incorporated more modern elements. There's a cracker throwing contest in Japan, a cell phone throwing competition in Finland, keg tossing in several locales, cow chip flinging in Beaver, Oklahoma (the Cow Chip Throwing Capital of the World since 1970) and just about anything else the imagination can conjure, including—but not limited to—mullet, toilets, watermelons, bowling balls, anvils, cars, pianos and large blocks of SPAM. Eureka, Kansas, hosts an annual "Hedgeball Chuckin'" in October, in which teams with everything from catapults to air cannons compete by firing hedge apples—the unripened fruit of the Osage orange—for distance.

Besides trying to see who could toss something the farthest, humans threw rocks, sticks or anything they could get their hands on to discourage predators from turning them or their families into lunch. They threw rocks, sticks and spears to turn some animal into lunch or dinner for them and their families. They also discovered that they could throw something to bring down an enemy, either the foot soldier who could be felled or the walls of his fortress. And that required inventiveness, the ability to devise a machine that could throw objects farther or could hurl larger objects.

It's those machines, designed for war, which became the basis for the engines used in the fun and games of punkin chunkin' which, at its essence, is no more than competitively hurling food. And, they're serious about it. The prize may be bragging rights and a gnarly wooden trophy but, deep down, this is war.

CHOOSE YOUR WEAPON

Pumpkins can be tossed by hand. Larry McLaughlin of Lewes thought that's what the first World Championship Punkin Chunk in Sussex County, Delaware, was going to be. The town of Morton, Illinois, does it as part of its annual Pumpkin Festival. But an 8-10-pound pumpkin, even thrown like a shot put, isn't likely to travel farther than 50-75 feet.

Pumpkins can be put into a bucket and either swung around the head and released at the right moment or whirled like a fast-spinning Ferris wheel at the side and tossed underhand. The gourd likely will beat the hand-tossed pumpkin, but still not travel far enough to suit the serious competitor.

What's a punkin chunker' to do? Since gunpowder and other explosives are out of the question, there's only one place to turn: ancient weapons that were powerful enough to punch holes in stone fortress walls. Except for the pneumatic cannons, introduced at the World Championship Punkin Chunkin' in the early 1990s, nearly all of the other punkin chunkin" machines are based—often loosely—on historic implements of war that relied on tension and torsion to power them, invented or modified by minds as ingenious as Leonardo da Vinci. The only way to appreciate today's machines is to understand the weapons of yesteryear:

SLINGS

Slings are probably the earliest effort to extend the range of a thrown rock or, later, a piece of baked clay or metal dart. Archeological evidence of slings is scant. It's usually the ammunition that's found. But a sling was recovered in an excavation of Tutankhamen's tomb, dating to the 1300s BCE. Another, dating to 800 BCE, was found in el-Lahun, Egypt.

The *Bible* mentions the use of slings in Judges 20:16, Chronicles 12:2, 2 Kings 3:25 and, of course, in the story of David and Goliath (1 Samuel 17:40, 49). Slings, though, seem to be one of those tools that developed throughout the world independently.

RIGHT: A woven sling from the Andes made of alpaca hair in the town of Lampa, Peru.
Photo by: Neil Grout

BELOW: Gian Lorenzo Bernini's statue of David in the Borgese Gallery in Rome, Italy.

BELOW RIGHT: Sketches of various types of sling (including a staff sling) by Leonardo da Vinci in his Atlantic Codex.

The key to the effectiveness of slings is that they're inexpensive to make, lightweight and, in the hands of an experienced slinger, can accurately hurl a small projectile from 220 to 440 yards.

Slings are usually a pouch in the middle of two equal lengths of braided cord. One cord has a loop that goes over one finger. The other has a knot that's held between two fingers that's released after the sling is whipped, usually underhand, toward the target. The Greeks, Romans, Egyptians, Assyrians and others found it an effective combat weapon. American soldiers in World War I even used slings to lob grenades.

An attempt to improve the sling was the staff sling. A wood staff as long as six feet was used as a lever. One cord of the sling was attached to the staff; the looped cord would slip from the end of the staff and the projectile would fly toward the target.

Staff slings were used more to heave larger rocks over the tops of fortifications.

The latest modification to the sling was the slingshot, developed in the late 19th century. A wooden or metal "Y" was fitted with two equal-length rubber cords with a pouch in the middle. Its range is about 100 yards. It's used mainly for target and small vermin shooting.

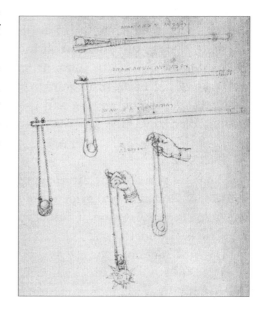

Slings became key parts of later and larger weapons and can be seen today on many punkin chunkin' engines.

BALLISTA

Ballista were mounted crossbows, introduced by the Greeks around 400 BCE. Some had laminated wooden arms, attached by twisted sinew. Others had two separate arms cocked back by twisted skeins. Cocked back, the wooden arms, bent by the tension created by the sinew, provided the power. They usually fired arrows or metal bolts but could be used to hurl small stones. Used until 1350 CE, they had a maximum range of 350 to 450 yards. Occasionally, the head of a dead enemy would be hurled into his camp as a warning to others.

BELOW: A Roman ballista.

BELOW LEFT: An onager.

CATAPULTS

The catapult was invented in 399 BCE in the Greek city/state of Syracuse. Simply, it was a long wooden arm with a basket or bucket on one end. The pivot point was at the opposite end. Cranking the arm—mounted in a twisted skein of rope, horsehair or human hair—created tension. When the trigger was released, it sprang forward, hurling the rock up and forward in an arc. Within 40 years, modifications had made it more powerful, relying on torsion rather than tension. Later catapults, in the realm of Julius Caesar, were used not only as heavy artillery on land, but also were mounted on platforms on Roman warships.

Torsion catapults could heave up to a 100-pound stone up to 400 yards. Sometimes catapults would be used to hurl dead cows or pigs over fortress walls, knowing that the rotting flesh could introduce disease into the enemy's camp.

Variants of the catapult included the mangonel and the onager, also called the "kicking ass" because of the recoil of the machine.

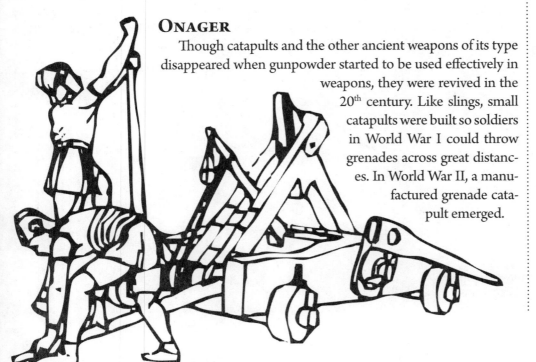

ONAGER

Though catapults and the other ancient weapons of its type disappeared when gunpowder started to be used effectively in weapons, they were revived in the 20th century. Like slings, small catapults were built so soldiers in World War I could throw grenades across great distances. In World War II, a manufactured grenade catapult emerged.

Trebuchets

Trebuchets—developed in China in the fourth century BCE and used in Europe between 850 CE and 1550 CE—superseded catapults, mainly because they didn't rely on torsion. The skill of making the skeins necessary to create torsion in later catapults had become a lost art over the years. Besides, trebuchets could be assembled on the spot instead of being wheeled over great distances to get to the front lines.

Trebuchets relied on slings to help propel large objects. A sling was attached to the end of a large wooden arm, much as they were attached to staff slings. The arm was mounted in a frame with the arm's pivot point about two-thirds to three-quarters of the way along the arm.

Initially, they were powered by as many as a hundred men pulling down quickly on ropes suspended from the short end of the arm. Later, they were fitted with heavy counterweights. Counterweight trebuchets could hurl a stone up to 600 pounds for 300 yards or more, whereas traction trebuchets (the ones pulled by hand) could lob a 100-pound stone up to 200 yards.

Spring Engines

Used only between 1050 and 1350 CE, the spring engine could shoot a small stone, bolt or arrow up to 250 yards. They relied mainly on the tension created by bending a light wooden arm, much like the power created when a sapling is pulled over.

For the most part, the advent of artillery powered by gunpowder put the catapults, trebuchets and all of their derivations out of business in the 14th to 16th centuries CE. Other than a few revivals in early- to mid-20th century warfare, they've become objects of study and sport by organizations that focus on medieval times. With explosives banned from Sussex County's punkin chunkin' competition right from the start, the teams who've competed every year since 1986 have turned to these ancient engines and whatever variations they can come up with.

ABOVE: A trebuchet.

RIGHT: A sketch of a spring catapult by Leonardo da Vinci in his Atlantic Codex.

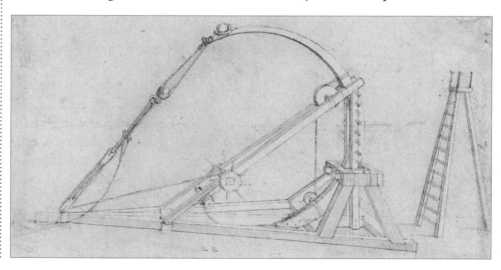

THE LEWES HAT STOMP

A blacksmith, an electrician, a plumber and a well digger were sitting in the blacksmith's shop one day talking about who could throw something the farthest. That's not the setup for a bad joke. It's more or less how World Championship Punkin Chunkin' got started in Sussex County, Delaware.

The standard story, with some literary license taken by the various reporters and others who've chronicled the event since 1986, is that blacksmith John Ellsworth, electrician Don "Doc" Pepper, master plumber "Trey" Melson and well-digging contractor Bill "Broad Dog" Thompson were sitting in Ellsworth's Preservation Forge Blacksmith Shop in Lewes sometime in October 1986 doing what guys often do: swapping lies and bragging. As the usual story goes, the four—all in their 30s—needed a new game to play. After deciding their old game of tossing anvils was getting to be too much to handle, they decided on building machines to toss pumpkins.

But the story with its multitude of variations isn't quite right. Thompson, Pepper and Ellsworth sat in lengthy, separate interviews in 2008 and explained what really happened that mid-October day 22 years earlier. Melson passed away in 2004.

The four men, who'd known each other for a while and had taken part in earlier challenges, often gathered at Ellsworth's blacksmith shop and house, as did others in their circle of friends. They were hard-working men who also played hard, partied hard and liked to have fun.

But the day the punkin chunkin' challenge was laid down, about two weeks before Halloween of 1986, the four weren't sitting in Ellsworth's shop talking about it. Pepper said he wasn't even there when the challenge was made. He was working that day. Ellsworth was alone in his shop. Melson and Thompson came in and the gauntlet—actually Ellsworth's hat—was thrown down.

There'd been other games played or discussed before then. At least some of the men had taken part in anvil tossing in the past, but Ellsworth said they'd not done it for five or six years: "It took us three or four days to recover from it." Ellsworth also had an idea for an elaborate set of Nordic Games involving climbing and throw-

ing axes and other manly stuff. They never came off. "I think we were just a little
too old, actually," Ellsworth said.

How they settled on punkin chunkin' as their next competition is a matter of
slightly differing memories.

Thompson said the idea for competing with homemade catapults was his. He
went to Melson's house to tell him and the two of them went to Ellsworth with the
plan and the challenge: "I seen this vision." He said Melson knocked Ellsworth's
hat off and Thompson stomped on it.

Ellsworth and Pepper said they'd been talking about punkin chunkin' for a little while before then. Ellsworth said Tina Thoroughgood and Tim Pfeiffer, two of the people in the crowd that hung around his shop, had seen or heard a news story about a physics class at a college in Maryland that had built a machine to throw pumpkins. Pepper and Ellsworth began making phone calls to try to find out more so they could go play, but came up empty. Ellsworth said Melson and Thompson came into his shop not long after; he told them about it, threw his hat on the floor and both men stomped on it.

As Pepper said, though, "I don't think the story of how it got started is as interesting as most of the people. Sometimes things just get started. They were just looking for something to do and have fun and competition."

"It's fun," Thompson said. "The inner child comes out."

Regardless of exactly how the challenge was made, the three who were there called some other "kids" to play. Ellsworth let Pepper know. They were to be a team. Thompson, paired up with Melson, also called his buddy Chuck Burton who teamed up with his brother Darryl.

Game day was set for the first Saturday after Halloween because pumpkins would be plentiful and cheap. The playing field would be at Thompson's place on Route 9 east of Georgetown near the area known as Gravel Hill, because he had the space.

They had just a few simple rules:

1. Pumpkins had to weigh between eight and 10 pounds.
2. Pumpkins had to leave the machine intact.
3. No part of the machine could cross the starting line.
4. No explosives could be used.

No one had much time to design and build a machine based on principles they weren't familiar with. No one had much money, so they built machines from salvaged and scrounged parts. No one expected it to become an annual event. And, as Pepper said, "Nobody was any good at it," though Melson and Thompson proved to be the best of the bunch.

The first Saturday after Halloween was Nov. 1. By the time the day arrived, word had spread. Thompson and Melson, Ellsworth and Pepper and the "Notorious Burton Brothers," as they'd become to be known, picked up another potential competitor: Larry McLaughlin. But McLaughlin, a Lewes municipal worker who knew some of the other men, didn't have a machine. In an interview in 2008, McLaughlin said, "Trey duped me a little. He said they were going to go out and throw pumpkins. I figured I could go out and throw pumpkins with the best of them by hand. That's what I thought it would be." But it wasn't. It was two spring-powered catapults and a large slingshot. It also was a huge party, with somewhere between 25 and 60 people and more than a few bottles of Boone's Farm Strawberry Hill wine. "If you said you didn't want any," Thompson said, "you weren't allowed in."

Melson's and Thompson's machine, mounted atop Melson's old International Scout, was laid out like a compound bow made of a gum tree cut down from Thompson's yard and powered by springs. Chuck and Darryl Burton used six garage door springs to power a hickory and white oak catapult mounted on a trail-

LEFT: The first chunk, 1986. Foreground: Bill Thompson's and Trey Melson's Scout-mounted catapult. Center: Chuck and Darryl Burton's trailer-mounted catapult. Rear: John Ellsworth's and Don Pepper's slingshot. Photo courtesy of Bill Thompson.

er usually used for hauling a tractor. John Ellsworth and Don Pepper strung large rubber cord between poles in the ground. "I didn't realize how stupid I was in those days," Pepper said. "I think we threw 17 feet the first shot; 25 the next." By the third shot, they got to 70 feet or so. The Burtons fared better, about 150 feet according to Chuck.

Thompson and Melson ruled the day. The arm on their machine kept breaking and getting shorter. Each time it did, their pumpkin went farther and farther. By the end of the day, they had won with a toss of 178 feet. Various publications over the years have listed the winning toss at everything from 50 to 187 feet. But Thompson said it was a measured 178 feet: "Not because I have a good memory. Because we argued over it." Today, though, the other competitors concede that it went that far.

Rumor has it that Larry McLaughlin managed to hand toss a pumpkin about 50 feet, but he also got to lay down a challenge of his own. He said he saw the "little contraptions" on the field and told Melson he probably could "build something to beat you guys. He (Melson) said, 'Bring it on.'" Everyone knew right away that there was going to be a second year. Thompson and Melson had won the bragging rights, and there was no doubt that a rematch was in order.

BELOW: John Ellsworth's belt sander dragster, named "Loco." Photo by author

"Once this gets into your blood," Thompson said, "you have to do it every year."

Besides, there seems to be something a little different in the blood of at least several of the early chunkers anyway.

Melson was described by Ellsworth as the "consummate gamesman." Capt. Harry "Speed" Lackhove, who'd known Melson since Melson was about 10 years old called him "mischievous," a description that apparently carried into adulthood.

Thompson, a cohort of Melson's, apparently had the same mischievous bent. According to the *Philadelphia Inquirer*, the two decided to take part in the four-day 100th anniversary of the Statue of Liberty in New York in July 1986. So, they took a Zodiac raft and joined the flotilla of Navy vessels, tall ships and private yachts anchored in the harbor. At night they camped on the beach of a bird sanctuary until authorities told them they couldn't. They toyed with taking their raft to Australia for the 1987 America's Cup, but didn't actually go.

Thompson, who said he weighed about 360 pounds back then, won Ellsworth's first anvil toss. Because he was sponsoring it, Ellsworth didn't compete, until Thompson needled him enough and offered him the prize money. Ellsworth, then, won.

Ellsworth also has gotten involved in belt sander drag races at Fenwick Hardware in Fenwick Island, Delaware, and in canoe jousting.

He's now involved in building and tweaking a lakester that he hopes will break the land speed record for a car with a conventional block engine.

With Pepper years ago, he modified a Jeep so it would run on freight train rail lines around Lewes. Pepper and he also got involved with building Soap-Box Derby cars for adults, more like two-man bobsleds on wheels, but couldn't find any place to race them.

Pepper started building model rockets a few years ago to figure out air currents. "I never played with model rockets when I was a kid," he said, "but they're kind of fun."

Melson, according to his mother Betty, bought a gyroplane and had it certified for flight. She said, though, he couldn't actually fly it because he was over the 200-pound weight limit for the aircraft.

Capt. Harry "Speed" Lackhove celebrated his 83rd birthday and hosted a fundraiser in 2007 by parasailing across Delaware Bay. He marked his 80th birthday by riding a motorcycle through a burning wall of wood. On May 15, 1998, he organized a "toilet toss" at his property on the Broadkill River, using specially designed "chunkers." For the future, Lackhove told *The News Journal*—a Wilmington, Delaware, newspaper—in May 2008 that when he dies he wants to be cremated and have part of his ashes injected into a pumpkin and shot into a field.

Lackhove and Ellsworth also are the fathers of the sport of street golf, a game with modified clubs that keep balls from lofting, using storm sewers as the holes. It's just the opposite of punkin chunkin', where lofting for distance is the goal.

A SMASHING GOOD TIME

I t isn't clear who, if anybody outside of Sussex County, heard the news, but 1987 was the year that punkin chunkin' unofficially went from a friendly backyard game to a world championship. After being on the winning team for the second year in a row, Bill Thompson stood atop a machine, declared the team "champions of the world" and challenged anyone anywhere to compete against them. But that year, it was still pretty much a quirky local event. They'd gotten some publicity in newspapers, enough—along with word of mouth—to draw about 200 spectators and five more machines to Thompson's field on Nov. 5.

The original three teams had had a year to improve their chunkers. The new entrants had had enough time to decide on designs they thought would take the crown, which actually were baseball hats for the first three finishers embroidered with "Pumpkin Toss '87." That also was the year they started naming their machines.

Trey Melson and Bill Thompson, still using Melson's International Scout as a base, went centrifugal. In an interview in 2008, Thompson said they continued to use the truck because Melson "was always wanting to be mobile, rapid fire." The centrifugal machine, named "Maximum Overdrive," created a little problem though. The wooden arm with a sling on it was mounted on one side of the truck and made it lean considerably when the 35-foot tall tower was collapsed so Melson could drive it to Thompson's house. Thompson said they had to put a pipe on the other side with a large safe hung on it to counterbalance the weight. The power from the centrifugal arm came from an eight-inch-wide belt than ran from one rear tire of the Scout to another tire mounted on an axle above it. To get enough tension to start the arm spinning, they put stick-um on the tire and Thompson held onto a rope.

John Ellsworth and Don Pepper completely scrapped their slingshot design and turned to a spring-powered machine that sort of shot the pumpkin along an I-beam. Sort of. Ellsworth said in 2008 that they went "brain dead" in the design. Pepper, in a separate interview, said they made a spring pack of several automobile coil springs stacked inside an old oxygen tank mounted on a trailer. The idea was to compress the springs with hydraulics, raise the I-beam and "let it go".

"What we didn't know," Pepper said, "was when you stack springs end to end,
they're only as strong as the weakest spring."

"'Doc' and I probably built more machines than anybody else (in the early
years)," Ellsworth said, "because we kept building machines that didn't work. It
was mostly my fault. I was pigheaded about it." Nevertheless, they were ready to
compete with the machine they called "Heavy Metal."

Chuck and Darryl Burton, calling their machine the "Notorious Burton
Brothers," stayed with the same basic trailer-mounted catapult design but instead
of having a large wooden crossbeam to stop the arm's travel, they decided on a
rope to halt its forward movement. It was a design element that proved to be trou-
blesome during the competition.

Larry McLaughlin, who'd told Melson the first year that he could build a better machine, showed up with "Larry's Toy," a spring catapult fashioned on a ladder

rack from a pickup truck and stuck in the ground. "The first shot," he said in an interview, "broke the arm in half. So he improvised by cutting down a hickory tree with a chainsaw and wrapping it with twisted nylon line to provide enough tension to fling it forward.

Harry "Capt. Speed" Lackhove, a retired schoolteacher and charter fishing boat skipper who was about 25 - 30 years older than most of the other chunkers, hadn't even heard about the first chunk until about six months later. But he decided to get in on the second contest with a slingshot mounted on an old boat trailer. He had garage door springs for power, hauled back by an electric boat winch. "Some brave soul had to reach out and cut the rope and let her go," he said in an interview in 2008. "It was not spectacular." Lackhove decided to get fancy and paint his contraption. The only paint he had available was yellow, so he named it "Mello Yello," a name that would stick through many evolutions over the next decade.

Lewes native Leon Fisher showed up with "Big Jack," a sewer pipe painted red, white and blue and propped up in the ground to look like a cannon. He and the other competitors were joined by a couple of other machines for which little information is available: "Penuel's Pitcher" and "Moose Gooser."

From their individual memories, some of the men who were there said Fisher's "cannon" wasn't a real cannon, but just a pipe with a lid on it. When the lid was removed, they said, out floated an orange balloon made to make people think it was a pumpkin leisurely making its way down field. However, a photo in *The Whale* newspaper in John Ellsworth's newspaper clippings collection shows Gus Nelson and Harry Howeth launching an orange balloon from a "cannon" in 1988. It doesn't matter much. Fisher was prone to similar jokes in subsequent chunks.

Nearly everyone who participated in the 1987 chunk described his own performance as everything from "abysmal" to "a learning experience." But the biggest learning experienced belonged to Chuck and Darryl Burton.

In an interview in 2008, Chuck Burton said his first mistake was not unhitching the trailer with the catapult on it from his 1978 GMC pickup truck. The second was partying too hard the night before. The third was letting a friend who was taking a captain's course tie a bowline in the stop rope. As soon as the cocked arm was let go, the knot in the rope parted and the arm, made of pressure treated lumber that year, smashed into the roof of the pickup truck. "I figure I had 550 pounds of energy (stored up)," he said. "I was tore up. I was inside trying to kick the roof up. I couldn't tell the insurance company anything." He and his brother continued chunking, but the best they could do was the pumpkin that flew out when the truck cab was smashed: 53 feet.

When it was all over, "Maximum Overdrive" outdistanced everyone else with a 496-foot chunk, according to two newspapers: *The Whale* and the *Delaware State News*. "Heavy Metal" was second with either 197 or 210 feet. The chunkers' memories aren't clear and none of them has any written records of that year. The newspaper accounts differ. "Larry's Toy" was third, with 156 feet.

Despite the whipping Thompson, Melson and team members John McQuay, Tom O'Hara and Rhonda McIntyre delivered to the rest of the field, Melson vowed to make 1988 even more spectacular. He told a reporter for the *Delaware State News*, "Next year we're going turbo."

When Nov. 5, 1988 arrived, his machine was turbocharged. So were most of the others. Every shot went into the woods. None could be accurately measured. Thompson said their machine had evolved into the "Ultimate Warrior," with the belt drive replaced by a chain drive. "We won," he said, "but they were fighting for second and third. Everybody thought 500 feet was a long way. We shot well over 1200 feet."

"If you look at the trajectory, " Ellsworth said, "ours should have thrown farther. They (Melson and Thompson) were throwing way up. Ours had a flat trajectory."

The Burtons and McLaughlin had a little controversy, too, for second and third places, as Thompson said. Trying to mark off where their pumpkins went, Chuck Burton paced off from his machine. McLaughlin had his young daughter pace off from his. Their steps, obviously, were different lengths. "He said, 'How much you got?'" Chuck Burton said with a chuckle. "I think 297. He said, 'I got 300.'"

There were six machines on the field that year. Thompson and Melson had their turbocharged centrifugal machine. McLaughlin had evolved into "Mishaps," a spring-loaded catapult. Ellsworth and Pepper, as Pepper said, got "a little smarter." They had the same trailer and I-beam, but added two six-foot arms that were perpendicular to the I-beam. Hydraulics pulled back the arms, which compressed coil springs. A sling-like device between the arms sent the pumpkin flying along the I-beam. Capt. Speed had another generation of Mello Yello.

The Burton brothers had worked some of the kinks out of their machine. The first out-of-state machine, a contraption from Philadelphia, joined them but Ellsworth remembers the team as one that "never successfully launched a pumpkin from beyond the tailgate of the truck."

The chunkers also were joined by a much larger contingent of spectators, 500 or more. Some of them, apparently hearing about it from friends, had driven from as far away as Ohio to witness the homegrown insanity unfolding at Thompson's field.

It was enough to make the original chunkers realize they couldn't handle it without better organization and a larger place to compete. Joe Hudson offered the field at the family's Eagle Crest Aerodrome between Lewes and Milton on Route One, and the chunkers started looking for someone to sponsor the event that had become an annual outing.

While the wheels were in motion to hold the 1989 chunk at Eagle Crest, a couple of early chunkers were turning their wheels in another direction. Chuck Burton said his brother Darryl decided he didn't want to play any more. Trey Melson, too, bowed out—at least for a while. After winning the first three years, he told everyone it was too easy and said he'd be back when the competition got tougher.

WHERE EAGLES 'N' PUMPKINS FLY

After Bill Thompson's challenge to the world two years before, the Sussex County boys decided the 1989 contest at Eagle Crest Aerodrome would end with the team throwing the farthest being anointed "World Champion."

It was still a free, one-day event mainly organized by John Ellsworth.

1989 also was the first public performance of the "Punkin Chunkin' Ballad," penned by Thompson shortly after the original contest in 1986. (See appendices for the song.) In 1989, Dawn Deschaine (now Dawn Thompson), added music to the lyrics. It's been performed nearly every year by her before each chunk since then as the World Championship Punkin Chunkin' Association's anthem.

Thompson may have gained some public glory with the song, but not with the chunk itself that year. With both of their main teammates bowing out of the competition, Thompson and Chuck Burton teamed up and, with the help of four or five others, built a large pine tree catapult on Burton's truck, with a 1000-gallon water tank to add some power. Thompson, in an interview in 2008, said, "It went negative feet." Actually, according to newspaper accounts of the chunk, the pumpkin went 54-and-a-half feet.

Harry "Capt. Speed" Lackhove decided to go centrifugal, a move that launched him into second place with a toss of just over 225 feet.

John Ellsworth and Don "Doc" Pepper, however, were the ones who really got it right. They modified the machine from the year before, which they renamed "Flipper," with 40 railroad car springs. "We had 100 tons of spring pressure," Ellsworth said in a 2008 interview. "It was the scariest thing I'd ever been around in my life.

"You couldn't put the pumpkin in until after you cocked it. You had to crawl up the arm to do it. You just envisioned it letting go while you were putting this pumpkin in and your hand disappearing with the pumpkin. We won with it that year and we cut it up, because neither one of us wanted anything to do with it."

Pepper attested to its scary nature. He also said that in the process of cutting it up and building "still another toy" after the '89 competition, they managed to snap the truck frame and reduce the number of axles.

The winning throw was 612 feet. It was Ellsworth's and Pepper's first throw. The other two turned into "Pie in the Sky," the term that chunkers use to describe a pumpkin that just turns into mush in mid-air because of the forces needed to launch it.

Rounding out the "unlimited" division was Team Maalox Moment, a group of eight men and women—including Leon Fisher—who managed to launch a

pumpkin just over 48 feet by jumping from the tailgate of a pickup truck onto what looked like a double teeter-totter.

Larry McLaughlin, improving his spring-loaded catapult, won the catapult division with a distance of 114-and-a-half feet.

With the ever-expanding newspaper publicity, nearly a thousand people showed up at Eagle Crest that year. With a crowd that size, the chunkers still were looking for a major sponsor and more organization. It wasn't to happen until 1991, the first year the Lewes Chamber of Commerce sponsored the event.

In 1990, the chunkers had more volunteers to help with the event, but they still were on their own. They did all the advertising and setup. Ellsworth was still the chief organizer, with local journalist Dennis Forney helping as the "unofficial" organizer.

Between 700 and 2500 people showed up to watch pumpkins and records smashed. (Three separate newspaper accounts differ and the chunkers don't have any accurate attendance records.) It was the first year that punkin chunkin' came close to being a threat to public safety. Thompson and Burton scrapped their hydro machine from the year before and went back to the centrifugal Melson-Thompson-designed "Ultimate Warrior." Overcoming some timing problems, the Warrior lofted a pumpkin 776 feet, exploding on the shoulder of southbound

LEFT: "The scariest thing I'd ever been around."—John Ellsworth. Photo courtesy of Don Pepper.

Route 1 and almost hitting a pickup truck parked there. Thompson also had an outlaw machine that broke all the rules. It was a stubby, mortar-like cannon with a six-inch bore, jammed into a tree stump and powered by black powder. It was just a joke, but a crowd pleaser nonetheless.

What wasn't a joke was "Ultimate Warrior's" 776-foot toss after two misfires. "Flipper," redesigned into a less scary machine, had its own equipment malfunctions and ended up throwing a pumpkin some 19 feet short of its previous year's record shot.

McLaughlin, who renamed his spring-loaded catapult "David the Giant Slayer" after mounting it on a dump truck, chunked out 200 feet. Lackhove's Mello Yello

RIGHT: The first "David the Giant Slayer" before it was mounted on a truck.
Photo courtesy of Larry McLaughlin.

BELOW: Centrifugals lined up at
Eagle Crest, 1992.
Photo courtesy of Don Pepper.

centrifugal machine tossed 374 feet. The rest of the nine-machine field consist-
ed of slingshots, catapults and a biplane. Joe Hudson, who was hosting the event,
decided to send up an airplane from which a pumpkin would be tossed when it
reached the starting line. "Twin Aero" had two false starts, then a 460-foot toss

Though they'd been doing it on their own and holding it as a one-day free event,
the punkin chunkers had been contributing to the local economy. Restaurants,
hotels and motels, service stations and other businesses in the area had benefited
from the Punkin Chunkin' spectators who needed a place to eat, a place to sleep
and a place to fill their automobile tanks. That may have been part of the reason
why the Lewes Chamber of Commerce decided to start sponsoring the chunk in
1991. In addition, it would provide some income for the Chamber. The Nov. 2,
1991 chunk was the first to charge for parking: $2 for cars and $1 for motorcycles,
and a $10 entry fee for the teams. For its part, the Chamber provided volunteers to
handle everything not involving the competition. The chunkers, with Ellsworth as
the organizer and liaison to the Chamber, took care of everything involving hurling gourds, including using a laser measuring device.

The Chamber, joined for a couple of years by the Sussex County Convention and Visitors Commission, was the chief sponsor for four years. Every year the Chamber sponsored the event, attendance increased dramatically: 5000 in 1991; 7500 to 10,000 in 1992; 8000 to 10,000 in 1993 in a cold, pouring rain; 20,000-25,000 in 1994.

Every year brought more teams, more inventiveness, new records and new "firsts," like the first all-female team, the first youth competitors and the first air cannon.

Every year attracted more national media attention, including ABC's Wide World of Sports and Good Morning America, CNN, NBC's Dateline, ESPN and Sports Illustrated.

Gov. Tom Carper in 1993 presented the World Championship Punkin Chunkin' with the Governor's Tourism Award as Delaware's outstanding special event. But there already were some seeds of discontent in the pumpkin patch, which would come to full bloom the next year.

Until then, though, the chunkers still were having fun, tweaking their machines or building bigger, badder and better engines in an attempt to grab the bragging rights and the rubber chicken that Ellsworth had spray painted gold and mounted on a board.

For at least a couple of years, Thompson's outlaw chunker was fired off in exhibition between the first two rounds of competition. Leon Fisher and a group of women called the "Punkinettes" got the honorary right to fire the first pumpkin

after showing up in 1991 with the Amazing Shrinking Slinging Machine. They put a full-size pumpkin into a hole in a box and took a pumpkin the size of a softball from another opening; then, fired it with a large slingshot. A pumpkin recipe contest was added in 1993, as were modest cash prizes.

A physics class from the Model Secondary School for the Deaf at Gallaudet University in Washington DC entered three machines in the first youth punkin chunkin' class in 1991.

A group of local women—Jane Thompson, Lynn Jones, Diane Zigman, Margie Brenneman and Leslie Mills—decided the testosterone-dominated sport should get a large dose of estrogen. They fielded the first all-woman team in 1991, calling themselves Punkin Machine Slayers, or PMS. Their flat-bed-truck-mounted catapult, according to Larry McLaughlin, had been his "David the Giant Slayer." McLaughlin and team partner J.B. Walsh were on to bigger and better things, with a surprise entry that year which later morphed into the centrifugal "De-Terminator," which took the record from "Ultimate Warrior" in 1992 with a chunk of 852 feet.

The next year, Ellsworth and Pepper abandoned "Flipper" and came up with what Pepper described as an air-powered crossbow named "Preservation Forge Under Pressure." They took the '93 world championship with the first official chunk over 1000 feet, an astonishing 1024 feet

But as the teams marched toward the 1994 contest, some of the fun seemed to be slipping. On Sept. 24, 1994, members of 10 teams representing 162 people sent a letter to the Chamber of Commerce threatening to strike if their list of 20 concerns and demands weren't met by Nov. 5, the appointed day of the chunk. They called themselves the United Pumpkin Chunkers Local 69 and had elected McLaughlin their president. Among their demands were no entry fees for past participants, a percentage of the profits to go to a local charity, enough portable toilets for the increasing number of spectators, no added classes of competitors and no more rules. They also wanted a better trophy.

Ellsworth, the liaison with the Chamber, said in an interview in 2008 that when the letter arrived, "At first we thought it was a joke. We had had a lot of practical joke applications come in. "When the PCU started up we thought

BELOW: De-Terminator, 1992 World Champion.
Photo courtesy of Larry McLaughlin

it was a joke, too." So much so that he responded with a joke of his own, a Sept. 27 letter to McLaughlin that said the Punkin Chunkin' Bylaws, which really didn't exist, required any threat of a strike to be accompanied by "form U812." The accompanying form—made up by Ellsworth—asked, among other things, "Have you or any member of your team ever been treated for mental illness?" It also asked if they thought O.J. Simpson was guilty, what their favorite color was and whether any of them could sing the Punkin Chunkin' Ballad a cappella.

But, Ellsworth said, it quickly became clear that the chunkers were serious. A meeting was held Sept. 29. All the points were discussed. When all was said and done, the chunkers decided not to strike. On Nov. 5, 1994, they were on the line: nine teams in the unlimited division, four in the youth under 10 years old, three in the 11-17 age bracket and six in the human powered class.

It was a year that proved to be a turning point for the annual competition:

First, the seeds of what soon would become a legitimate association with a charitable bent had been sown with the formation of the United Pumpkin Chunkers and some of its demands. The registration fee collected from the teams in 1994 went to Boy Scout Troop #2540 for their assistance in setting up and helping to run the show.

Second, it would be the last year of Chamber of Commerce sponsorship. Though the chunk would stay at Eagle Crest Aerodrome for three more years, it would be with a new sponsor. By 1994, the chunk was the largest of four annual events sponsored by the Chamber. The chunkers insist that they were dissatisfied with the Chamber's sponsorship and broke it off. Chamber President Wayne Leatham told the *Cape Gazette*—a Lewes, Delaware, newspaper—in February 1995 that the Chamber already had voted unanimously to drop its sponsorship. According to the newspaper story, Leatham said it had become too much to handle and that the Chamber had met its goal of attracting large numbers of post-season tourists to the resort area. Under the Chamber mantle, the event also had become a community-wide effort. The City of Lewes, Lewes Volunteer Fire Company, Milton Chamber of Commerce, Cape Henlopen High School Volleyball Team, Lewes Lions and Rotary clubs and a host of others had joined the ever-growing list of volunteers.

Third, after sitting out since his third straight winning year in 1988, Trey Melson rolled back into competition in 1994 with a machine that literally blew away the competition. "Universal Soldier," a camouflage-painted air cannon atop an SUV on a truck frame, shot a 10-pound pumpkin 2508 feet, nearly a half mile and more than twice the record set by Ellsworth's and Pepper's "Under Pressure" the year before.

HEAVY ARTILLERY MOVES IN

When Trey Melson came out of self-imposed retirement in 1994 and drove "Universal Soldier" onto the field at Eagle Crest Aerodrome, he ushered in a new era in punkin chunkin.' His machine, a camouflage-painted 4x4 "Jimmy" on a deuce-and-a-half frame with a nearly 40-foot smoothbore cannon made from 16-inch steel pipe on top, had nothing to do with the ancient siege engines that were the basis for nearly all the other chunkers.

It was a piece of heavy artillery powered by a compressed air tank that developed 500 pounds of pressure. It wasn't the first machine to use compressed air. John Ellsworth's and "Doc" Pepper's "Under Pressure" crossbow used air to drive a piston that powered their machine to a world record the year before. It also wasn't the first air cannon, just the first one to catch everyone's attention.

In 1993, locals Charles "Bruv" Sockriter, Mike Hazzard, Eric Quigley, Jerry Donahue, Ed Vickers, Clint Fluharty and Allen Linton built an air cannon in three days, called it "Oops! There it Goes" and took it to the chunk. It didn't do well.

Mike Hazzard said in a 2008 interview that some of them had gone to a couple of chunks before that as spectators. Their entry into competition happened by accident. He said Sockriter, who installed tank fields for service stations, had been testing a 10,000-gallon tank with four pounds of pressure. Instead of bleeding off the air, he hurriedly unscrewed the cap and just that little bit of pressure "blew the cap out of sight." So, with about a $500 budget, the men took an old aboveground tank and fitted it with a 10-12-foot metal barrel and a ball valve.

They tested it late at night just days before the chunkin' contest on a narrow mile-long field on Hazzard's land in Angola, west of Lewes. "Next thing we hear sirens coming from everywhere," Hazzard said, and turned around to see "probably six or seven state police cars and the S.W.A.T. team." Someone had called the police because they thought they "were under attack or something." The S.W.A.T. captain asked the men what they were

ABOVE: A later version of Universal Soldier.
Photo courtesy of Terry Brewster.

FAR RIGHT: First air cannon.
Photo courtesy of John Ellsworth.

doing and when told, "punkin chunkin', he said, 'What?' So, we all stood around and tried the chunker," Hazzard recalled, "so they knew what we were doing."

At the chunk itself an equipment malfunction kept the cannon from shooting any great distance. To keep pressure behind the pumpkin, they'd fitted the barrel with a piece of foam wadding on a metal plate, attached to a chain to keep it in the barrel. The chain broke and the wadding was launched with the pumpkin. Since the wadding became the forward-most piece of the machine, as per the rules, the measurement was taken from the wadding to the pumpkin instead of from the barrel to the pumpkin. (Wadding now is strictly prohibited.) Hazzard doesn't remember how far it went, but is convinced they would have won if the measurement had been from the barrel to the gourd.

That was it for them. Sockriter gave the barrel and tank to Chuck Burton's sons to help them get into the game, and it was later reborn in the youth division. Hazzard said he helped Larry McLaughlin for a few years on his "De-Terminator" centrifugal machine, but the rest of the first air cannon crew didn't really get into punkin chunkin'.

Harry "Capt. Speed" Lackhove, in an interview in 2008, said Melson was at the '93 chunk as a spectator and told him afterward, "I'll tell you how to build one and win the chunk." Lackhove said he told Melson it was beyond his expertise and stayed with his centrifugal "Bad to the Bone – Son of Mello Yello".

Melson's son-in-law, Eric Nelson—who later wound up on Melson's team because he "married into the family"—said in an interview that his father-in-law had been toying with the idea of an air cannon before seeing the Sockriter/Hazzard cannon. "He'd say, 'Look how far you can shoot a pea through a straw' or 'Look how far you can shoot a wire nut through a pipe.'" Melson built his cannon, which he told reporters took him four days to build from junkyard parts. Air cannons today can cost upwards of $100,000 and often rely on major sponsors to help keep them competing.

Lackhove got into cannons later. So did other people. Out of 96 entries in the 2007 World Championship Punkin Chunkin', just under a third were air cannons. Since 1994, catapults and centrifugals have exceeded Melson's 2508-foot throw, but air cannons still domi-

Not Everybody Likes "Air"

Air cannons changed the face of punkin chunkin' because of their sheer power. They're crowd pleasers but have their critics. Some people complain that they can't see the pumpkins in the air. Others say air cannons have produced a lopsided competition.

World Championship Punkin Chunkin' Association President Frank Shade disagrees. He said the right combination of mechanics and wind could lead to an air cannon being out-chunked by a catapult, trebuchet or centrifugal machine.

"Bad to the Bone," captained by Donny Jefferson, has been the first-place centrifugal machine every year from 1996 through 2007 and holds the world record for its class: 2770 feet.

"Bad to the Bone".
photo courtesy of Jim Riley, Team PumpkinHammer.

The 3/4s of a Mile Club

"Old Glory".
photo courtesy of Jim Riley, Team PumpkinHammer.

"Old Glory," captained by Joe Thomas of Lewes, is among only six punkin chunkin' machines to exceed the 4000-foot mark. All of the 4000-foot-plus chunkers are air cannons.

"Aludium Q36 Pumpkin Modulator" from Illinois was the first reach the milestone in 1998. "Old Glory" from Delaware hit the mark two years later and again in 2004. "Second Amendment," the Michigan cannon that holds the world record of 4434 feet, did it in 2003, 2004 and 2005. "Big 10 Inch " from Delaware, Pennsylvania and New Jersey and the Delaware cannons "Y ask Y," and "Bad Hair Day joined the elite club in 2005. "Big 10 Inch" exceeded the mark again in 2007.

When "Trey" Melson rolled his "Universal Soldier" air cannon onto the field in 1994, he chunked nearly twice as far as the next most powerful machine, John Ellsworth's pneumatic crossbow "Under Pressure." Since then, other machines have been closing the gap. The air cannon "Second Amendment's" record chunk is 1.5 times farther than the record-throwing catapult "Fibonacci Unlimited II" from Massachusetts.

nate the farthest reaches of the playing field. "Second Amendment," an air cannon from Howell, Michigan, holds the distance record of nearly 7/8s of a mile.

With air cannons in the picture, the chunkers expanded their competition classes in 1995 to separate them from the other unlimited machines. That was the first year that the Roadhouse Steak Joint on Route 1 became the chunk's sponsor and the event expanded to a two-day affair. It also was the year that the chunkers got a better trophy, the gnarly wooden one that exists today. There were small versions of it for the individual class winners and the large traveling trophy for the overall champion. Bill Thompson said in a 2008 interview that local chainsaw carver Danny Beach, a chunker himself, made them.

After watching Melson the year before, Lackhove decided that maybe he should go the air cannon route. He talked with his team. Most of them decided they wanted to stay with the centrifugal machine. "Don Jefferson Sr., " Lackhove said in a 2008 interview, "told me 'I don't want to have anything to do with any kind of blowgun.'" So, the team kept "Bad to the Bone" and Lackhove gathered some other guys together to build the cannon called "Mello Yello VIII – New Matik Pumpkin Planter." It was a good move for Lackhove. He took the record from Melson with a 2655-foot chunk. He also took home the newly made wooden trophy and a $2500 prize.

Melson congratulated Lackhove. But, according to newspaper reports of the event, Melson's team had used up a lot of compressed air the day before by putting

BELOW: Mello Yello VIII.
Photo courtesy of Larry McLaughlin.

FAR LEFT: "Ultimate Warrior,"
1994.
Photo courtesy of Don Pepper.

ABOVE: Old Glory – Ultimate
Warrior team, 1996.
Photo courtesy of Bill Thompson.

LEFT: The retired "Ultimate
Warrior" in Bill Thompson's
yard, waiting for someone to res-
urrect it.
Photo by author.

BELOW: "Aludium Q36 Pumpkin Modulator". Photo courtesy of Bill Sharp

on a rapid-fire demonstration of multiple pumpkins. On the day of actual competition, they discovered that Melson's son-in-law Eric Nelson had forgotten to re-fill the air tanks that morning, so they only had enough power to chunk 2240 feet. Nelson's wife Trish—Trey Melson's daughter—said in an interview that her husband had overslept because he'd gone home to help her. She was pregnant with their third child and had been sick.

Air cannons began to appear on the scene in increasing numbers on a year-to-year basis. The Bottle & Cork bar and club in Dewey Beach, for example, had fielded a cannon named "Top Secret" in 1995, which finished third. Melson kept improving on "Universal Soldier." Lackhove came up with other generations of "Mello Yello." Lewes resident Joe "Wolfman" Thomas fielded the "Old Glory" team in 1996 that, for a while, was basically the same team that fielded Bill Thompson's centrifugal "Ultimate Warrior."

Thompson later retired "Ultimate Warrior" and came up with the "Road Warrior" cannon.

Eventually, "Second Amendment" from Howell, Michigan, joined in the fun, as did "Big 10 Inch" with its multi-state team and a number of other guns that now compromise nearly a third of the punkin chunkin' field.

But the one that really set the Sussex County boys back was a big cannon from Morton, Illinois, that ended up being the first machine to take the coveted traveling trophy out of the state of Delaware.

Word had spread in 1996 that a super-secret cannon named "Aludium Q36 Pumpkin Modulator" was on its way to Eagle Crest to take part in the competition. Publicly, the Sussex County crowd said a collective, "Bring it on!" Privately, they may have worried some, but maybe not. The air cannon, which cut its teeth in an exhibition at its own town's Pumpkin Festival a month earlier, was pretty much shrouded in secrecy.

ABOVE: "Aludium Q36 Pumpkin Modulator", looking down the length of the barrel toward the compressed air tank. Photo courtesy of Bill Sharp.

"Aludium Q36"—a takeoff on the name of an explosive that the Warner Bros.' Looney Tunes cartoon character Marvin the Martian threatened to use to blow up Earth—was born at Parker Fabrication, a family-owned industrial machine shop in Morton. Matt Parker, vice president of the company, his father Pat, and Chuck Heerde, Jim Knepp, Rod Litwiller, Rick Campbell and Steve Young made up the team. According to details available only after the World Championship Punkin Chunkin' that year, they'd built a cannon with an 80-foot-long barrel and a laptop computer-driven system that monitored air pressure, temperature, valve opening and other key data. The team also relied on trajectory and velocity calculations from an engineering faculty member at Bradley University in Peoria. Word was that despite having a barrel that could break down into three parts, the machine was so massive that it was placed under time and speed restrictions on the Pennsylvania Turnpike.

Once in Delaware, the Illinoisans picked up another member: Bill Sharp, a Milton, Delaware, excavating contractor. Sharp said in a 2008 interview that the Aludium team had called a Caterpillar dealer near Lewes to see if anyone had a large air compressor. The dealer had recently sold a new Caterpillar backhoe to Sharp and the salesman gave them Sharp's phone number. Sharp, who'd never taken part in a chunk before, was thrilled to become their gas-passer.

"They got all set up," he said. "I pulled in on a Friday night after work. All the locals gave me a hard time. I said, 'These are the only guys who ever asked me to play. You guys never asked me come out and play.'"

RIGHT: The "happy" Punkin'
Chunkin' trophy, 1998.
Photo courtesy of Bill Sharp.

"Aludium Q36" won that year with a record 2710-foot shot and took home the traveling trophy. In newspaper interviews, the team always said that the key was how the air was stored in the tank. Sharp, in the 2008 interview, said the secret was "dry air." Air heats up as it's compressed. As it expands it cools down and creates moisture. Sharp said he figured out a way to heat the tubes that the air passed through on its way from the compressor to the tank to keep the moisture from forming. That, he said, created more power.

Of course, there was some controversy. This is, after all, punkin chunkin'. According to a number of chunkers who were there, Trey Melson had been delaying his shots, waiting for the wind to die down as it usually did in late afternoon. By the time the final shots were fired in the competition, it was getting dark. Melson's pumpkin couldn't be found.

The decision was made to have the judges search anew the next morning. Aludium Q36's pumpkin was found and measured. Melson's pumpkin wasn't found. Aludium was declared the winner. Pumpkin pieces, presumably from Melson's cannon, were found in an old chicken coop on the other side of Route 1, but that was a few days later and too late.

The next year, the Illinois boys returned, and left the trophy in Melson's hands. Melson had sworn in 1996 that his missing pumpkin had gone more than 3000 feet and should have won. In 1997, his record shot was 3718 feet. It was found and he did win.

In 1998, with the chunk under a new organization at a new field north-north-east of Millsboro and southeast of Georgetown in an area known as Hollyville, the trophy again went away to the Prairie State but part of the trophy was missing. Aludium Q36 had a record-breaking toss of 4026 feet. Melson's' pumpkin wasn't found. There were rumors, even accusations, that Melson hadn't loaded his cannon. He was adamant, and more than a little annoyed, and said he did but that the spotters who searched until dusk just didn't go far enough or look long enough. Pieces of a pumpkin were found in the trees at the far end of the field the next day.

When Punkin Chunkin' Association members went to Melson's house to pick up the trophy and deliver it to Bill Sharp, the local member of the Illinois team, it was deformed. Melson, soured by both '96 and '98, had taken a saw and cut off its face. Sharp repainted it and put a Smiley face on it. He also repaired some wood rot. The year Lackhove had the trophy, he displayed it proudly in the front yard of his Lewes home by burying the base in the soil. Eventually, the trophy's face was handed over and carefully reattached with long screws.

The air cannon trophy and the world record trophy returned from Illinois in 1999 to a team with members from Delaware, New Jersey and Pennsylvania. "Big 10 Inch," with a 100-foot-long aluminum barrel and a 10-inch bore, wiped out the Illinois team and everyone else with a chunk of nearly 3695 feet. The next year, "Big 10 Inch" was disqualified from the competition. The cannon had fired 4114 feet, the longest in the chunk's history at the time. The reason for the disqualification, according to the *Cape Gazette* newspaper in Lewes, was that one of its tanks had been topped off with helium for a practice shot, which was a violation of the rules that had to be established when air cannons started taking to the field. According to the newspaper, "Big 10 Inch" appealed, saying all of its tanks had been inspected and approved by Punkin Chunkin' Association officials before the

BELOW: Margie Brenneman, a member of the first all-female team (right), stages a mock protest at the 1994 chunk on behalf of the pumpkins hurled through the air and smashed on the ground.
Photo courtesy of John Ellsworth.

actual competition and had been cleared to compete. But the board maintained that they were in violation of the rules and awarded the trophy to "Old Glory" and its 4085-foot shot. The appeal letter from "Big 10 Inch" co-captains Pete Hill of Alloway, New Jersey, and Ralph Eschborn Jr. of Chadds Ford, Pennsylvania, sought a shootout with "Old Glory." The local cannon's Captain Joe Thomas was willing to, for a friendly wager, but the association wouldn't approve it.

"Big 10 Inch" accepted the ruling and came back year after year, ending up with the air cannon division trophy in 2007 with a shot of more than 4211 feet.

The World Record, for not only the division but overall, however, belongs to "Second Amendment" from Howell, Michigan: 4434 feet, reached in 2003. According to its website, "Second Amendment" has reached more than 5000 feet in test firings. "Aludium Q36" fired 4491 feet in Morton, Illinois, on Sept. 19, 1998, and was entered in the Guinness Book of World Records. In 2001, it hit 4860 feet, again in Illinois. But as far as the World Championship Punkin Chunkin' Association is concerned, it doesn't matter: The only shots that count are the ones fired at the annual competition in Sussex County, Delaware.

And for most of punkin chunkin's years, the shots were mainly fired by backyard engineers who would marvel at their and fellow chunkers' inventions with sounds that would rival the grunts of comedian Tim Allen's character "Tim 'The Tool Man' Taylor."

WOMEN AND CHILDREN FIRST

Women and children weren't the first to chunk pumpkins, unless you count the years when the kids might have thrown a piece of pumpkin pie from their highchair trays. But they've always had some role in the annual contest. Punkin chunkin', despite being a male dominated pastime, has been very much a family affair nearly from the start.

The children of chunkers grew up watching their grandfathers, fathers, uncles, other male relatives and family friends pour hours of their spare time into devising and building ways to hurl gourds at an annual competition. Realizing that to have a future punkin chunkin' needed to rely on the next generation, the chunkers decided early to encourage the kids. "We fought tooth and nail for youth groups to build their own machines," Chuck Burton said in an interview for this book. In 1991, the first youth division entered the field.

Adult women wouldn't get their own division until 2007, but, like the children, they'd been involved in at least a peripheral way from the beginning. Some, as individuals, would load pumpkins into machines or pull the triggers that would launch the gourds. Most, though, were support personnel, mainly keeping an eye on the kids, running for parts for the machines and keeping the crews in the pits fed. In 1988, during the third chunk, Trey Melson's mother Betty and sister Terry made pumpkin pies and sold them for a dollar a slice from the porch of Bill Thompson's home. And Betty Melson, in a 2008 interview, admitted she helped bankroll her son's machines through the years.

Many women just considered themselves "punkin chunkin' widows." There were a couple that some people consider the first all-women teams. Lewes character Leon Fisher had the "Punkinettes" in 1991, but they were mainly a novelty group who did things like launch tiny pumpkins with a slingshot. "Capt. Speed" Lackhove had a contingent of women associated with his "Mello Yello" team in the late '80s, but Lackhove said in a 2008 interview that they were his "cheerleader girls," grown women dressed in yellow ponchos and carrying pom-poms.

ABOVE: Some of "Capt. Speed's girls.
Photo courtesy of John Ellsworth.

The first all-women team was actually "PMS" in 1991. Margie Brenneman of Lewes said in a 2008 interview that she and Lynn Jones decided the year before that they should get involved in actually chunking. They were joined by Diane Zigman, Jane Thompson and Leslie Mills and got started with Larry McLaughlin's and J.B. Walsh's old dump-truck-mounted catapult "David the Giant Slayer."

"We had a pine tree log (for the catapult arm), " Brenneman said, "and a spaghetti strainer for the pumpkin basket." They wore pink sweatshirts and pink hardhats. "We named it 'PMS' because that's what women get," Zigman said in a separate interview. It was also an acronym for "Pumpkin Machine Slayers."

Men teased them all day. "We gave it right back to them," Brenneman said. "Obviously," Zigman said, "we weren't serious competition. The guys were moving on to more sophisticated methods. We already knew we weren't competing. We were just having fun."

"We busted a few pumpkins," Zigman said. "We had one good throw, not very far." Newspaper accounts said the "good throw" was 93 feet, good enough, Brenneman said, for a third-place among catapults.

Zigman and Brenneman were on the team only that year: But other women joined the team—Dawn Stephens and Kristi Patterson—and "PMS" continued, with Thompson as captain, to compete for two more years.

It would be several years more before another all-women team appeared. "Bad Hair Day," the first all-women air cannon team, debuted in 1998. Stephanie Coulbourne of Milton, one of the current co-captains and Punkin Chunkin' Association secretary for the past five years, said in an interview in 2008, that the idea started two years earlier when she, Cindy Wright, Michelle Harris, Melissa Jefferson and other women were declared "non-essential personnel" and kicked out of the pit area when the chunking competition started.

"We had set up and were taking care of feeding everyone in the pit area," she said, "but when it came time to throw, we had to leave and stand under a tent until they were done. We didn't think that was fair."

They began talking about it, came up with a plan, talked with their husbands—all chunkers—about their idea, and started working on an air cannon. Why a cannon? They didn't want to compete against machines like the centrifugal "Bad to the Bone" that Coulbourne's and Jefferson's husbands belonged to. It already had finished in the top three in 1994 and 1995 and has taken first place among centrifugal machines every year from 1996 through 2007. "We didn't want to come in and compete against them and take the championship," she said. "We wanted to play, too." Besides, she said, Trey Melson—who'd brought in the first serious air cannon—started small and kept growing.

Wright worked at Bad Hair Day? (The question mark is part of the name.) and salon owner Drexel Davison became their prime sponsor for most of their years on the field. Hudson Truck and Trailer Repair in Harbeson, where Coulbourne's husband works, gave them the dump truck that became the base for their 40-foot, 10-inch-bore barrel, though Coulbourne pointed out that it needed some work: "It came from a junk yard and had a tree growing up through the engine compartment."

Wright and Jefferson had a plan to pump air for the cannon from another truck, an old septic pumping truck that was donated by someone else.

The women did, and still do, all of the work except welding. By the 1998 chunk, they were ready to go. Their first chunk was about 60 feet and very black. Some of the male chunkers said in interviews for this book that the reason was that the septic pumper hadn't been completely cleaned out. Coulbourne said it was because

BELOW: "David the Giant Slayer," With modifications, the catapult became "PMS." © 1991, William L. Brown. Reprinted with permission.

they couldn't get enough pressure by pumping air from the truck through hoses to the cannon. Their best shot that year was just under 498 feet, 12th place out of 13 air cannons. Over the years, though, they've made modifications to the cannon, including replacing the septic pumper with a tank mounted directly on the cannon. They've earned the distinction of being among only six cannons to shoot a pumpkin more than 4000 feet, taking 3rd place overall in 2005 with a chunk of 4060.97 feet.

Coulbourne said that chunk—putting them in the company of "Aludium Q36," "Second Amendment," "Old Glory", "Y ask Y" and "Big 10 Inch"—went a long way toward earning them the respect of the predominantly male teams in a predominantly male sport. In the early years, she said, "They thought we were a joke for a while. Having the septic truck didn't help either."

In 2004, a second all-women air cannon team emerged: "Let's Bounce," captained by Connie Sisson of Milton, Delaware. Its barrel blew apart on the first shot. It didn't compete in '05, but another all-women team did: "Dragon Lady," captained by Gina McConnell of Preston, Maryland.

With three teams in competition in 2006—the minimum number required for a new division—the women lobbied the Association for their own class. It happened in 2007. "Let's Bounce," "Dragon Lady" and "Bad Hair Day" competed as the Female Air Cannon Division, finishing in that order. Coulbourne said they wanted to "level the playing field," even though "Bad Hair Day" already had shown it could hold its own against behemoth air cannons with barrels of 100 feet or longer.

Coulbourne said besides being able to "go out there and pull with the boys," the women are now "accepted by them." That's important, she said, as important as the fact that her young children are becoming curious and learning about the machines and, maybe someday, will carry on the tradition.

Terry Brewster, Trey Melson's sister, said in an interview in 2008 that her three-and-a-half-year-old grandson will captain his own team—with proper adult supervision, of course—at the 2008 World Championship event: a trebuchet named "Pumpkin Seed." Brewster said her grandson attended his first chunk in utero, knows all of the machines by name and is fond of yelling, "Fire in the hole."

Michael Nelson, Trey's grandson, finished his last year in the youth air cannon division in 2007 with a second-place shot of 3028 feet. Michael's "Ozone Blaster" finished first in the division in 2006 with 3718 feet and third in 2005 with 3052 feet, after having competed with a trebuchet before then.

His mother Trish, Trey's daughter, said her children were so into chunkin' that one year—even though their parents told them not to—they decided to practice with the trebuchet at the family's home near Georgetown when their parents weren't home. The trebuchet, as they're sometimes wont to do, fired backwards and the five-pound weight they were using as ammunition blew out a window frame of the house.

Jake Burton, whose father Chuck and uncle Darryl had one of the three original machines in 1986, is another child of the chunk. Born the year after that first competition in Bill Thompson's field, Jake said his earliest memory of punkin chunkin' was as a young child riding in the cab of "Ultimate Warrior," the centrifugal machine that dominated the early years.

BELOW: Another example of a woman's machine. Dawn Thompson's "Bust-O-Matic" catapult and its backstop. Photo by author..

When he was nine years old, with "no help from Dad," the youngster decided he wanted to compete. Joe "Wolfman" Thomas, who already was fielding the "Old Glory" air cannon, and fellow chunker Frank Payton taught the youngster how to weld. Starting with a base built on the air cannon built by Charlie Sockriter, Mike Hazzard and crew in 1993, "Young Glory" was born. It debuted in 1997 in a pouring rain, Jake Burton said in a 2008 interview, and fired 630 feet to take the Youth 11 and Under class trophy. By the next year, with modifications, Jake and his team were not only competing in the annual Sussex County event but were traveling to chunks elsewhere, like Morton, Illinois, and Busti, New York.

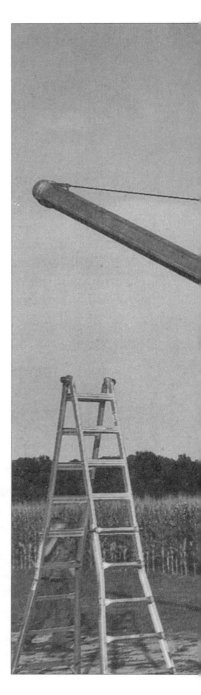

Having years earlier changed to a barrel bore of eight inches so he could fire larger pumpkins than required in the youth division, Jake Burton and team shot more than 3945 feet in the 2003 World Championship Punkin Chunkin' in Delaware, nearly 300 feet farther than his mentor Joe Thomas over in the adult air cannon class. Moving to the adult class himself in 2005, Burton finished 10th out of 20 cannons, came in fourth in 2006 and finished second in 2007.

Jake Burton and Trey Melson's and Terry Brewster's grandsons weren't the first, nor are they the only, kids to be drawn into punkin chunkin' simply through exposure to it.

The men who dominated the sport made room early for younger participants not only to make room for their offspring, but also because the whole process of punkin chunkin' is the ultimate science project. According to the *International Journal of Pumpkin Tossing* published in 1991 by John Ellsworth's brother-in-law and well-known illustrator William L. Brown, a high school science teacher in Reno, Nevada, had discovered the value of punkin chunkin' as a teaching tool independent of the annual Sussex County, Delaware, event and had held a contest limited to students at the school at least a year earlier.

When they added a Youth Division in 1991, organizers of punkin chunkin' issued a public challenge to schools, especially engineering departments at colleges and universities, to try their hand at beating the backyard wizards of Slower Lower Delaware at their own game. First to take up the challenge was a physics class from the Model Secondary School for the Deaf at Gallaudet University in Washington, DC. The students' "Lean Green Catapulting Machine" set the first youth record with a chunk of 91 feet.

By the following year, teams from Cape Henlopen High School in Lewes and Sussex Technical High School near Georgetown had entered the youth fray. The rest, as they say, is history. By 2007, there were six youth air cannons, with the top gun ("Snot Rocket" from Federalsburg, Maryland) firing more than 3200 feet; two machines in the youth human powered class, eight youth catapults, seven youth trebuchets, three in the youth 10 and under catapult class and three in the youth 10 and under trebuchet division competed. In the years between 1991 and 2007, various schools and youth groups have entered the annual contest, from universities like Delaware, Maryland and Tennessee to middle schools and high schools from Delaware, Maryland and other states. In addition, schools have taken up the

ABOVE: Michael Nelson works on "Ozone Blaster" before a chunk.
Photo courtesy of Trish Nelson.

RIGHT: Jake Burton's "Young Glory III."
Reprinted with permission; World Championship Punkin Chunkin' Association.

BELOW: Some of the next generation. The "Sister Slinger" team.
Reprinted with permission; World Championship Punkin Chunkin' Association.

punkin chunkin' mantle on their own. For example, Dutchess County Community College in Poughkeepsie, New York, sponsored a local chunk for eight years for Hudson River Valley students; West Springfield High School in West Springfield, Massachusetts, has its own annual competition, and the physics club at Elon University in Elon, North Carolina, raised $100 and 90 food items in a charity chunk there in 2007.

Boy Scout, Cub Scout, Girl Scout and Brownie troops from all over also have entered the field throughout the years. The learning value to scouts has led to the formation of "NJ Hurl," an organization that has set up a chunk patterned after the Sussex County event, planned for Bader Airfield in Atlantic City, New Jersey, for the first time in fall 2008. It's geared toward scout troops, church organizations and schools. The goal, according to its website (http://www.njhurl.com), is to contribute all proceeds to the Boy Scouts of America and raise money for camper scholarships. The World Championship Punkin Chunkin' Association has worked closely with the "NJ Hurl" organizers and is actually sanctioning the event.

The importance of youth participation in punkin chunkin' was publicly noted in a Nov. 16, 1994 letter from John Ellsworth to the editor of the *Coast Press*. The lengthy public "thank you" to everyone involved in the chunk that year, Ellsworth noted, "One of the many fun aspects of the day is watching the youngsters compete in the varying youth classes as well as the human powered class.

"Their imagination in building machines is what this event is all about." Ellsworth singled out eight youth teams that year, from Virginia, Maryland and Delaware.

The educational aspect of punkin chunkin' also hasn't escaped the attention of those who've been chunking in Delaware for more than two decades. When the chunkers began transforming themselves into a charitable organization in the mid 1990s, they began by establishing and handing out scholarships to science and engineering students.

SWEET CHARITY

Aside from the first few years, which were huge adult tailgate parties, punkin chunkin' has pretty much been a family affair. And since at least the mid-1990s, it has been a charity event. The seeds for their charitable bent were planted in 1994 by the 10 teams who formed the basis for what later would become the World Championship Punkin Chunkin' Association, an incorporated non-profit organization. Though a donation was made to a local Boy Scout troop in 1994, the first charitable donation of any size was made the following year.

When the chunkers and the Lewes Chamber of Commerce parted ways after the 1994 event, the fledgling United Pumpkin Chunkers had to find another major sponsor. According to Larry McLaughlin, the organization was approached by two businesses in Dewey Beach but both proposals were for hurling pumpkins into Rehoboth Bay, making the chunk more a show than a competition.

The chunkers also were approached by Wallace P. "Pete" Townsend with a proposal from his Roadhouse Steak Joint near Lewes in the area known as Midway. They liked it, especially the part that put all of the responsibilities for the event on the Roadhouse. All the chunkers had to do was take responsibility for the rules governing the machines themselves and, according to a rough draft provided by then-president Larry McLaughlin, "Show up and have a good time." Among the line items in the proposal was $12,000 for charity. When the 1995 chunk was over, however, $18,000 was donated to 21 organizations. Among them were Special Olympics; Children's Beach House; Rehoboth, Lewes and Milton Little Leagues; Delaware Hospice; American Leukemia Society, and Pennsylvania Industries for the Blind and Handicapped.

When the Roadhouse took over prime sponsorship, it expanded the chunk to a two-day event, added entertainment ranging from hot air balloon rides to carnival rides to live bands of national scale like the Drifters, The Coasters and the Marvellettes. McLaughlin said in 2008 that the Roadhouse sponsorship didn't equate to a lot of money in Townsend's pocket but meant a lot to his business to have its name associated with the already successful tourism event. Between 25,000 and 30,000 spectators watched the chunk that year, despite high winds and low temperatures. From then through 1997, when the power of the chunkers' machines outgrew the Eagle Crest Aerodrome field, crowds of at least 20,000 showed up each year in all sorts of weather, including torrential downpours. The admission and parking fees, the registration fees from the chunkers, vendor fees and donations from individual businesses helped increase the amount donated to charity each year.

The Roadhouse sponsorship ended when the chunk moved to William T. Hurdle's 225-acre soybean field at Sussex routes 305 and 306 near Millsboro in 1998. But the charitable aspect of the chunk continued under the chunkers' own mantle. Though the World Championship Punkin Chunkin' Association (WCPCA) seal showed up as early as 1995, the association itself didn't incorporate and become a certified non-profit organization until 1998. That was the year that Bill and Dawn Thompson, through his company B&B Mechanical, became the chunk's organizer, promoter and prime sponsor so that it could continue after the Roadhouse sponsorship ended. Bill Thompson was Punkin Chunkin' Association (PCA) treasurer and B&B Mechanical became the headquarters for the chunk. Thompson told the *Cape Gazette* in September 1998 that he was getting 40 phone calls a day and only five had anything to do with his well-digging business. The rest were punkin chunkin' related. The Thompsons were the primary organizers through the 2000 chunk. According to a combination of PCA financial reports and newspaper accounts, the chunkers gave away $10,000 to $12,000 in scholarships each of those years and $2,000 to individual organizations like the Southern Delaware Keepers of the Promise, which handled parking and tickets.

In 2001, the year the annual punkin chunkin' expanded to a three-day event under a reorganized association, the chunkers distributed more than $70,000 to scholarships and various community organizations, most of them youth-based. In 2005, more than $80,000 was distributed, including $10,000 to St. Jude Children's Research Hospital. In three years, the World Championship Punkin Chunkin' Association had donated $45,000 to St. Jude and it continues to contribute annually to the research hospital. WCPCA President Frank Shade said in a 2008 interview that he's been involved in fund-raising for St. Jude for nine or ten years, but the motion to include St. Jude as a major beneficiary of punkin chunkin's donations was made by John Collier at one of the association's business meetings. Shade also said the association with St. Jude was what led to the Charlie Daniels Band becoming the first major country music act to headline at punkin chunkin'. Shade said Daniels, also involved with St. Jude, slashed the band's appearance fee dramatically to headline the 2005 Friday night concert at the chunk. Other beneficiaries in 2005 included the Lower Delaware Autism Foundation and the Shriners Hospitals for Children.

By 2007, with the chunk at yet another location—Dale Wheatley's farm near the intersection of routes 404 and 18 near Bridgeville—and attendance estimated at 60,000, the chunkers raised more than $80,000 for charities and scholarships. Plus, every group that volunteers to help with things like setting up snow fencing or handling parking at the vent receives a donation based on the number of hours the volunteers put in.

The association votes on which charities receive the bulk of the donations. In addition, according to association secretary Stephanie Coulbourne and treasurer Terry Brewster, the top three finishers in each category get to nominate their favorite charities, which receive funds based on the distances those teams' pumpkins are chunked.

"Chunkers," Trish Nelson (Trey Melson's daughter) said in an interview, "really are more focused on the kids and charities."

"The ideal," Shade said, " is to give them (a charity like St. Jude) a check that they turn around and say, 'We don't need it; we fixed all the problems; give it to somebody else.' Are we there yet? No. Is it possible? Probably not in our lifetime, but every dollar helps."

Shade considers the World Championship Punkin Chunkin' Association as two distinct operations. One is the chunk itself and all the logistics involved. The other is the business end, with the business being to raise as much money as possible for worthy non-profit organizations. He said the WCPCA is operating in the black, with enough money in the bank to pay all the upfront costs of getting the chunk going—like insurance, fencing, tents, entertainment and everything else involved in setting up—so it can hold the chunk, replace the money for the next year and raise money to donate.

"I'd like to see this organization have a million dollars in assets," he said. "If you ever stop chunking, at five percent, you'd have $50,000 a year that you could donate to your scholarship programs and to charities."

For a few years in the mid-1990s, chunkers got not only bragging rights, hats, trophies and rings for winning tosses, but modest prize money was handed out. That stopped when the chunkers reorganized into the charitable association they are now. A few years ago, Shade said, one of the corporate sponsors offered to put up $10,000 as prize money to be divided among the various chunking divisions. The proposal was taken to the board and the trustees and, unanimously, they rejected it.

"Chunkers are very generous people," Shade said. "They have no problem giving away the money they raise."

ABOVE: The World Championship Punkin Chunkin' Association relies heavily on a number of sponsors to help make the annual event possible. The home page of the association's web site, http://www.punkinchunkin.com, contains links to many of those sponsors.

CAN I HAVE YOUR AUTOGRAPH?

If pop-culture icon Andy Warhol had ever met a punkin chunker, he never would have predicted in 1968 that everyone, at some point in their lives, would be world famous for just 15 minutes. Punkin chunkers may have started as local characters proud of referring to themselves, as the Burton brothers did, as "notorious," but their fame has endured for more than two decades.

They've become like rock stars with hearts.

Eric Nelson, Trey Melson's son-in-law and sergeant at arms of the World Championship Punkin Chunkin' Association, said he was on a service call at a Bethany Beach business in June 2008. A woman in the store said, "You're Eric," even though he didn't have a name tag on his shirt. Nelson said she then expanded her recognition: "You're with punkin chunkin.'"

Nelson's late father-in-law probably had even more name recognition, as did many of the other early chunkers. Trey Melson, Bill Thompson, John Ellsworth and "Speed" Lackhove have been interviewed innumerable times by local, national and international media. Several times they were the prime focus of newspaper and magazine stories. Trey's mother, Betty Melson, said she didn't remember the year, but recalls asking her son one day who he was talking with for so long on the telephone. His answer was "Japan."

Over the years, calls came in to individual chunkers from all over the world. Reporters from national publications like *Sports Illustrated* and crews from national radio and television programs showed up at the annual Sussex County event, including ABC's Wide World of Sports, Good Morning America, CNN, NBC's Dateline and ESPN. The Discovery Channel in February 2003 ran an hour-long documentary that most chunkers say was responsible for the explosive spectator interest in the annual event. Chunkers who were featured on the Discovery Channel documentary have said they're recognized on the street.

In June 2007, WCPA President Frank Shade and his wife Billie Jo, a member of the all-women air cannon team "Bad Hair Day," were on the Montel Williams show as part of a segment on unusual events around the country.

One of the Trebuchet Stars

"Yankee Siege" from Greenfield, New Hampshire, has dominated the trebuchet competition since 2004 and holds the trebuchet record of 1702 feet. The team is not only proud, but also humble and realistic about its top-dog status.

"Yankee Siege"
photo reprinted with permission of Steve Seigars.

"Winning is only a temporary condition," the team says on its website (http://www.yankeesiege.com). "Sooner or later somebody will beat us."
The team sees that potential "somebody" as the trebuchets "Trebabaric" from Washington state, "PumpkinHammer" with its Delaware, Maryland, Pennsylvania and New Jersey team, and "Merlin/King Arthur" from Virginia. Plus, the website says, "There is always the potential that some unknown could arrive on the scene. In 2004 'Yankee Siege' was unknown."

British television's Channel 4 sent a crew to the 2005 chunk to film the performance of an entry built by the British TV show "Scrapheap Challenge," a contest program that had been on the air since 1998 in which teams competed against one another in various engineering challenges.

Five years earlier, Bill Thompson actually traveled to England and was there as a technical consultant and special commentator for the filming of an episode of "Junkyard Wars," the British-produced American version of the show. Thompson was there in 2000 for a challenge titled "Ballistic Missiles" which aired in the U.S. on January 3, 2001. Two teams competed by building machines—a trebuchet and an air cannon—and chunked pumpkins at a target 50 yards away.

Over the years, individual chunkers and their teams have been invited to travel to other locales to lend their expertise to new sites that want to hold chunks, to take part in charity chunks, even taking part in commercials. "Yankee Siege," for example, was asked to shoot a commercial in April 2008 for a company that makes monitors for the power industry. The Greenfield, New Hampshire, trebuchet—which has held the record for its class every year since 2004—has been visited by a group of teachers on behalf of a museum planning a trebuchet exhibit. It also rents itself out for corporate and public events.

Radio stations in towns near the homes of some of the machines have sponsored events over the years with the local chunkers becoming the draw. Though the year is hazy in her memory, Terry Brewster recalled a radio promotion in Baltimore involving her brother's air cannon "Universal Soldier." After getting a special permit to cross the Bay Bridge, the camouflage-painted air cannon wound its way to Baltimore where it delighted crowds by firing pumpkins up a hill on the outskirts of town. Her brother, she said, let just about anybody—especially children—pull the trigger and feel the thrill of firing the cannon. When it was over, she said in a 2008 interview, they got lost and ended up driving the massive military-like vehicle past Camden Yards as an Orioles game was about to get underway. She said the baseball fans waiting to get into the ballpark, at first, were taken aback; then, got a real kick out of seeing the machine on the street.

In 1996, Harry "Capt. Speed" Lackhove was featured in the syndicated "Ripley's Believe It Or Not" newspaper feature for his record chunk of 2,655 feet with his "Mello Yello" air cannon the year before.

From 1997 through 2001, the chunkers contributed to their own celebrity status by having trading cards of each team made. The "Acme Catapult Co.", a central Illinois catapult that finished first in its class in Sussex County in 2000 and second in 2002 and 2003, showed its catapult in action on a 2007 wall calendar.

Though they've held onto their minutes of fame for years, not every chunker's experience with the limelight has been positive. In 1995, John Ellsworth, "Doc" Pepper and the rest of the "Under Pressure" team were invited to New York City to tape a segment for "The Late Show With David Letterman."

The idea started with Chris Joker and Stephen "Ace" Shelton, two morning personalities at radio station WZBH in Georgetown at the time. Their intent was to convince the late-night talk show to send a crew to the chunk itself. They sent letters and beach paraphernalia to the production crew and capped it off by sitting in the audience once wearing pumpkin hats to try to get attention. It worked, except

BELOW: "Under Pressure" on the road.
Photo courtesy of John Ellsworth.

the show decided to mix the fruit and have the punkin chunkin' machine go to the Big Apple. About two dozen people—the "Under Pressure" team and a contingent of supporters—hitched up the 50-foot-long pneumatic crossbow to a truck driven by a professional, loaded up two vans and headed to New York for the taping on October 31, just a few days before that year's chunk.

After navigating the city streets, they set up on 53rd Street and got ready for the taping, a few of them playing a little street golf to kill time.

Ellsworth, to this day, feels "used by David Letterman." Other chunkers, some of whom were in New York that day and some of whom read about it in local newspapers, express the same sentiment. They say that Letterman never came out to the street, never mentioned Delaware, never mentioned punkin chunkin', and just made a reference to a couple of crazy guys who'd built a machine to throw pumpkins. The "Under Pressure" team, used to throwing for distance, was restricted to 300 feet and was told to try to chunk a pumpkin into the trunk of a New York City taxi. They came close, but couldn't quite do it. Ellsworth said a member of Letterman's crew, eventually, threw a pumpkin into the cab's trunk from a ladder to make it look as though "Under Pressure" had hit its mark.

The Delaware contingent also was annoyed that the TV show's crew made them take down signs they had made thanking the businesses and individuals who'd helped them get their machine to New York.

At the annual chunk that weekend, the "Under Pressure" team found support from their fellow chunkers. Bill Thompson had bought an old car for $100, the chunkers leaned a large white sign with David Letterman's name on it against the car and, when the competition was over, used it for a target. Trey Melson, after missing the sign with a few launched pumpkins, hit the gas on "Universal Soldier" and ran over the sign and the car too.

A few years later, after the Illinois air cannon "Aludium Q36" won the world championship twice, they too were invited to the Letterman Show. Bill Sharp, the Delaware member of the Illinois team, said in 2008 that they fired into the Hudson River toward New Jersey and had no problems with the experience.

In 2003, "Acme Catapulting Co." made it onto "The Tonight Show with Jay Leno" in Hollywood and used their pumpkin-launching machine to hurl kitchen appliances as a Sears energy-saving appliance promotion.

In June 2008, writer/producer/director Costa Mantis added to the chunkers' celebrity status with the release of the feature documentary "Flying Pumpkins: The Legend of Punkin Chunkin." Mantis and his crew spent a year following 20 punkin chunkin' teams from several states to put together an 88-minute film that debuted at a theater in Leesburg, Virginia. In keeping with the chunkers' philanthropic bent, he's donating part of the proceeds from the sale of DVDs (http://www.flyingpumpkinsthemovie.com) to St. Jude Children's Research Hospital.

FAR LEFT: "Under Pressure on 53rd St.
Photo courtesy of John Ellsworth.

BELOW: Hitting the target.
Photo courtesy of John Ellsworth.

GROWTH SPURTS

Since it started in 1986, punkin chunkin' has grown almost immeasurably in a number of ways. Chunkers as a whole have grown from a handful of backyard mechanics out just to have a good time at a big party into members of a major philanthropic organization that also contributes significantly to local tourism.

Individual chunkers, though still at their core a bunch of big boys with big toys, have acquired knowledge that, at first, was foreign to many of them. "Doc" Pepper, one of the original chunkers, said in an interview that he is "amazed how dumb I was when I started and how much I've learned over the years.

"I know how to throw spit balls. I know how many RPMs a golf ball spins coming off a driver because I've tried to make pumpkins spin that way. I know how fast a five-inch shell spins coming out of a Navy gun on a ship. I've learned a multitude of things about ballistics and air dynamics and springs and steel types and tensions and sheer strengths on bolts."

The allure of the challenge to hurl pumpkins farther and farther has drawn in people with backgrounds in engineering and mathematics and related disciplines and has led to the evolution of machines that can launch pumpkins at speeds of 400 miles an hour or more without disintegrating them midair most of the time. (A pumpkin that disintegrates before it lands is known as a "Pie in the Sky" and doesn't count in scoring the distance.) Their acquired knowledge about how to hurl farther than the next team has resulted in machines that periodically have outgrown the playing field.

The first few machines to compete outgrew Bill Thompson's field in just three years because they'd become powerful enough that the pumpkins didn't land until they were in the woods.

The increasing number of machines with constantly improving designs also had to move from the next venue, Eagle Crest Aerodrome on Route 1, partly for the same reason. By 1997, the last year at Eagle Crest, they were shooting onto and over Route One, shooting into the parking lot of Lewes Church of Christ some 3000 feet from the firing line and shooting into the woods. They also had to move because the event itself had gotten too large for the site. Joe Hudson, whose family had allowed the chunkers to use their field at no charge since 1989, told local newspapers that they were starting to get complaints from neighbors about four-wheelers looking for errant pumpkins in neighboring fields.

William T. Hurdle's bean field near Long Neck became the chunkers' home field in 1998. It was more than 5000 feet long, more than enough distance for any machine throwing a perfectly straight line. But there still were pumpkins lost in the woods. It wasn't the machines' power or the ever-increasing size of the crowds that led to the next move, however. It still was growth, though. In 2005, Hurdle's field was sold to a developer, setting off a scramble for a new site for the following year. The chunkers got a last-minute reprieve and didn't actually have to move until 2007, but the search for a suitable new location almost resulted in the annual event moving to another state. Recognizing the tourism dollar value of the World Championship Punkin Chunkin', both Worcester and Wicomico counties lobbied hard to get the annual event to move over the state line to Maryland. Other proposals came in from locations in Kent County, Delaware. In the end, though, the punkin chunkin' association firmly believed the annual contest was a Sussex County event that should stay in Sussex County. State Rep. Joe Booth of Georgetown tried to help. He wrote a letter to Gov. Ruth Ann Minner on the chunkers' behalf and suggested that the state buy a nearly 400-acre parcel south of Georgetown that was about to be put up for sale by Townsends Inc. poultry company. Booth thought it would provide a permanent home for the annual punkin chunkin' and preserve open space. Association President Frank Shade said in a 2008 interview that the property had a $20 million price tag that no one could justify spending. Delaware State Economic Development officials did consider leasing a site for the event but couldn't find any landowners in Sussex County willing to take part because they were concerned about crop damage and liability issues. In the end, the association reached an agreement with Bridgeville officials and Dale Wheatley to use the Wheatley family's nearly 1000-acre farm to keep the chunk in Slower Lower Delaware.

Growth in punkin chunkin' also came in another form: The world outside of Delaware took notice and took part. As the annual event garnered more publicity outside of the area, people started traveling from other states to watch and to compete. Shade, who admitted that "Eighty percent of all statistics are made up on the spot," said that "Ninety-five percent of the people who come to punkin chunkin' are hooked for life, either as spectators or because they think they can build a machine to beat the others. The other five percent say, 'I think we passed an outlet (store) someplace.'" That's how a number of chunkers got started.

Rich Foley, for example, went to a chunk with his family in the early 1990s. A few years later, he was part of a Boy Scout troop that competed with a trebuchet. In 2001, the Newark, Delaware, resident and two friends from New Jersey and Pennsylvania were punkin chunkin' spectators and immediately formed a team to start building what they refer to as "PumpkinHammer – The Great American Trebuchet." Their first competition in 2002 brought them a third-place finish in their division. The multi-state entry, which also includes team members from Maryland, finished in the top three every year except 2006 and is one of the first

LEFT: "Pumpkinhammer."
Courtesy Jim Riley, Team
PumpkinHammer

two trebuchets to throw more than 1350 feet. The "PumpkinHammer" team redesigned their machine for the 2008 competition to "The World's Largest Whipper," an all-steel machine with a whipping action to the arm.

Bruce Bradford, owner of S&G Steel Erectors in Howell, Michigan, which built the air cannon "Second Amendment," had a similar beginning. In 1998, he read a news story about the Delaware contest and decided to go to see what it was all about. He posed as a newspaper reporter to get into the pit area close to the other

FAR LEFT: "United Flingdom II."
Reprinted with permission, World
Championship Punkin' Chunkin'
Association.

guns. The next year, "Second Amendment" entered the field and finished fifth. By 2002, the cannon's more than 3881-foot shot set a world record and the team took the world championship trophy home to the Wolverine State. The following year, it set another record—more than 4434 feet—that still stands.

In addition to those two machines and the plethora of entries from Delaware's neighboring states of Maryland, Pennsylvania, New Jersey and Virginia over the years, punkin chunkin' has seen an influx of other competitors from the Great Lakes region, New England and the South. The 2007 competition saw the multi-state air cannon "The Big 10 Inch" take the champion adult air cannon division. The adult catapult "Fibonacci Unlimited 2" from Weymouth, Massachusetts, walked away with its division trophy. "Yankee Siege" from Greenfield, New Hampshire, took the adult trebuchet title. The two New England machines hold world records, set in 2005, for their divisions. "Roman Revenge" and Onager," both from North Carolina, finished in the top three in the adult torsion catapult class. "Mischief Knight" from Arlington, Massachusetts, and "Pumpkin Slayer" from Durham, North Carolina, were in the top three in the adult human powered class.Other competitors from outside the Mid-Atlantic region over the years have included the Morton, Illinois, air cannon "Aludium Q36 Pumpkin Modulator," the first to take the world championship trophy out of Delaware; the Central Illinois catapult "Acme Catapult Co.;" a high school entry called "Jack-O-Launcher" from Canfield, Ohio, and the air cannon "Honey Dew Screw" from Kingston, New Hampshire.

But the machine that traveled the farthest to get to Delaware was "United Flingdom," a centrifugal machine from England that entered the competition in 2005. "United Flingdom" was born on Channel 4 in England on the TV show "Scrapheap Challenge." The program, forerunner of the U.S. show "Junkyard Wars," pits four-member teams against each other in competitions involving engineering and ingenuity. For the 20th year of the World Championship Punkin Chunkin', the producers decided to enter the Delaware competition with a machine built by a team of men who'd shown their mettle on previous shows.

In just a few days, the "Scrapheap All-Stars," as they were called, built a centrifugal machine from an old bus frame, a crane, hydraulic rams and an old axle. Power to spin the rotating arm at about 200 miles an hour came from an old six-cylinder bus engine and transmission. They crated it and, after some concerns from the U.S. Department of Homeland Security, shipped it to the states. It was damaged in shipment and the British team had to scramble with makeshift repairs to their engine.

When the competition came, they were up against venerable favorites and seasoned machines like "Bad to the Bone" and "De-Terminator," both of which had placed in the top two positions in their division for years. Larry McLaughlin's "De-Terminator" had equipment problems and ended up with two "no throws." Its third launch became "pie in the sky." Don Jefferson's "Bad to the Bone," had three throws well over 2000 feet and took the trophy with a 2704-foot heave. "United Flingdom" had a 1355-foot throw on its first attempt, followed by two "pie in the sky" heaves. It was good enough to give the British a second-place finish in the division and some good television for the folks back home.

When the chunk ended, local teams began bidding heavily for the British entry. It was sold to the Yanks and refurbished. In 2007, with Jeffrey Wheatley of Bridgeville, Delaware, as team captain, "United Flingdom II" finished second to "Bad to the Bone" in the centrifugal class. "De-Terminator" came in third.

With various machines entering the Delaware contest over the years, it's only natural that the sport itself has caught on in other locales. The contest that appears to have been going on the longest—other than the world championship in Delaware—is in Morton, Illinois. When the Lewes Chamber of Commerce was the prime sponsor of the Delaware chunk, the Morton Chamber of Commerce contacted its First State counterpart to find out how it could incorporate punkin chunkin' into its annual pumpkin festival. Morton, between Peoria and Bloomington, was designated the "Pumpkin capital of the world," by then-governor James Thompson in 1978. The town is the home of the Nestlé/Libby's pumpkin processing plant and produces more than 80 percent of the world's canned pumpkin. Morton has held a fall pumpkin festival since 1967 and, in 1996, added punkin chunkin'. When the Chamber of Commerce decided to sponsor the chunk, it challenged local backyard engineers to design machines to compete. The Morton contest was nearly cancelled in 2007 because the Chamber of Commerce pulled out, saying there were so many similar events around the country that the big machines needed to attract large crowds weren't as available. But the Jaycees, Kiwanis, Morton Business Association and other organizations stepped in to keep the chunk going.

Not all punkin chunkin' events that have cropped up over the years have endured. Some, like the Busti Fire Department fundraiser in Busti, New York, and the punkin chunkin' that started in 1999 at the York, Pennsylvania, Fairgrounds aren't held any more. But others have begun. For example, the Youth Garden

Project in Moab, Utah, started an an-
nual "Pumpkin Chuckin' Festival in
2007. There's a "Pumpkin Chuckin'"
weekend at Clark's Elioak Farm in
Ellicott City, Maryland, in early
November. The Spencerville Fair in
Spencerville, Ontario, Canada, started
a September punkin chunkin' in 2006.
Other chunks include Raleigh, North
Carolina; Bristol, Connecticut; Aurora,
Colorado; Mauston, Wisconsin, and
Nekoosa, Wisconsin. For people who
want to travel farther, the European
Punkin 'Chunkin' Championship start-
ed in Bikschote, Belgium, in 2004.

LEFT: Getting ready to fire in
Belgium, 2004.
Reprinted with permission, World
Championship Punkin Chunkin'
Association.

Though anything hurled at another event doesn't count toward the world championship, chunks in other states have given punkin chunkers a chance to travel,
show off, maybe pick up a trophy or two and fine tune their machines in prepara-
tion for the annual Delaware event. They've also given the chunkers a chance to
just fool around.

After "Aludium Q36" took the world championship trophy back to Illinois in
1996, the newly organized chunk in Morton gave the Sussex County boys a chance
to hit the road. Five teams traveled to Morton for the 1997 chunk there and came
back with a hostage. Frank Shade said they kidnapped "Aludium's" stuffed "Martin
the Martian" doll and, on the way back to Delaware, stopped to take pictures of
it in various places. They sent the photos to "Aludium's" team and, eventually, returned the mascot itself.

Shade said there isn't quite as much travel as there used to be. He said the price
of fuel is helping keep a lot of chunkers closer to home. He also said the evolution
of some of the big machines makes set-up difficult. Some take a couple of days to
set up, and some of the teams cannot take off work long enough to go elsewhere,
set up, compete, tear down and head back home.

If they're not traveling to other states as much, though, they are making time to
get to Delaware each fall.

CAUTION! FALLING PUMPKINS!

As machines' power increased and punkin chunkin' grew from just three hurling engines to a hundred at the annual Delaware event, the organizers had to adopt measures to protect the chunkers and the tens of thousands of spectators who began showing up each year. In 1986, there were just four rules. In 2007, the eighth revision of the rulebook was 23 pages long, mainly because of safety regulations. There's "zero tolerance" for anyone who breaks the safety rules. Among the rules are mandatory safety meetings for team captains each morning of the competition.

Punkin chunkers have known from the start that the machines they built could be dangerous, both on the field and off. Sometimes, some of the players who've been at it a long time chuckle when they say something like, "Remember the year when Chuck Burton smashed the top of his pickup truck?" or "Remember when the piston blew out of Trey Melson's cannon and pieces landed between two parked cars?" But deep down, they know that anything can happen, any time, and they're constantly trying to keep the danger in check.

From the time larger crowds started showing up at the chunk, the chunkers had to keep reminding spectators to not stand right behind the machines at the firing line because any catapult or trebuchet is as capable of firing backward as it is forward. Any piece of any machine is capable of flying off. The arms of the large centrifugal machines are spinning at 100 miles an hour or more. Pumpkins come out of air cannons at more than 400 miles an hour and the tanks that power them can contain up to 2,000 pounds of pressure. Any machine is capable of misfiring and shooting a pumpkin that goes straight up instead of out. Even firing the way they're supposed too, a crosswind can catch a pumpkin and make it slice or hook.

When punkin chunkin' was at Eagle Crest Aerodrome, the organizers developed a layout intended to keep spectators behind the firing line but off to the sides. Nevertheless, a few errant pumpkins flipped into the crowd and flew out over Route 1. The Delaware State Police periodically closed the highway when the big guns fired in 1997. Pumpkins also have smashed on the shoulder of the road, nearly hit a pickup truck, smashed into the

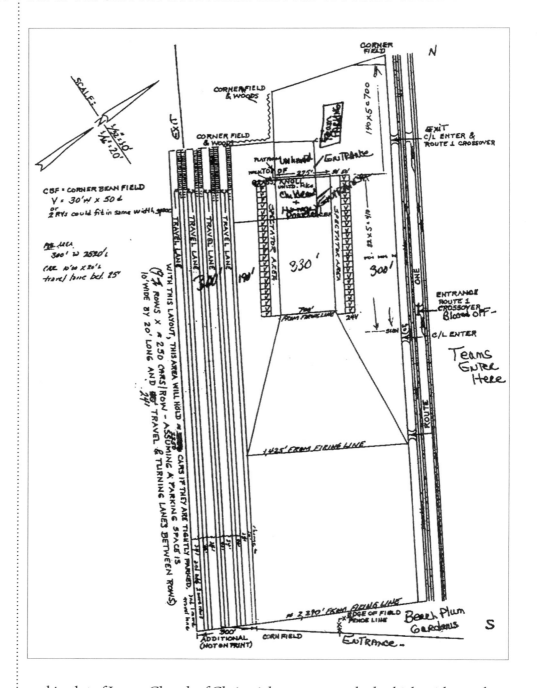

parking lot of Lewes Church of Christ right next to a parked vehicle with people in it, hit a van with a dog inside and hit a duck in flight. Luckily, other than the duck, no one was hit.

Larry McLaughlin's record-setting shot of 852 feet with his centrifugal machine "De-Terminator" in 1992 landed in the crowd and also managed to not hit any of the spectators.

In 1997, "Old Glory" was being towed to the chunk and became unhitched from the tow vehicle. The barrel brushed by a Milton man and knocked him into the pond where he was fishing. He wasn't seriously hurt.

In 1999, after his son Jake had come back from competing in Busti, New York, Chuck Burton was helping spruce up "Young Glory."

ABOVE: Part of the crowd at Eagle Crest Aerodrome with a clear area behind the machines. Photo courtesy of Larry McLaughlin.

Chuck Burton, in an interview in 2008, said he was spray painting the tower. His nephew said one of the rachet tensioners that holds up the barrel looked loose. As soon as Jake touched it, Chuck Burton said, "It was just like someone shooting a crossbow at me. It beat into my skull. I lost my memory for a year after that."

At the 2004 chunk, the barrel of the air cannon "Let's Bounce" blew apart when the big gun fired. Nobody was hit.

In Greenfield, New Hampshire, in 2007, Chuck Willard—a member of the "Yankee Siege" team—was knocked unconscious for a couple of minutes when the 55-foot-long boom of the trebuchet kicked up and hit him in the chin when it was being lowered to reload a pumpkin. Steve Seigars, the team captain, told the New Hampshire Union Leader that something in the trigger mechanism apparently didn't catch properly.

Chuck Burton said his accident made him "push safety a lot harder on myself and everybody else." Bill Sharp also began pushing for more safety. Both are on the safety committee that was formed in the late 1990s. Co-founding chunker Bill Thompson also is among the 13 members of the committee that inspects each machine and certifies it to compete each year. The safety committee began drafting rules that changed over the years as situations developed and organizers modified the layout to keep spectators close enough to see the action but far enough away to protect them from harm.

In 2003, the state of Delaware expressed safety concerns, especially over the big air cannons. There were meetings and legal opinions about jurisdiction, but when all was over, the state began requiring all of the cannons' pressure tanks to be built to American Society of Mechanical Engineers (ASME) standards, to have ASME approved pressure relief valves and to be inspected and certified by the Delaware Division of Boiler Safety. The provision added to the cost of the cannons, but most of the earlier cannons had tanks made from just about anything, some of them not really designed to be pressurized containers.

The state requirements were in addition to elements the chunkers themselves already had added, like a provision forbidding the use of PVC pipe for cannon bar-

Count Your Fingers

John Ellsworth and Don Pepper called their spring-powered "Flipper" an incredibly scary machine because someone had to crawl up the long metal arm to load it after it was cocked. Other punkin chunkin' machines potentially fall into the same category. Catapults and trebuchets, for example, have to be cocked before the pumpkin is loaded into the sling, basket, or other receptacle. Rules that weren't in existence when "Flipper" was on the field, however, require safety straps or other mechanisms to guard against premature firing. Air cannon rules require that the pumpkin be loaded before the air tank is pressurized to guard against a several-hundred-mile-an-hour pumpkin taking off someone's head.

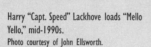
Harry "Capt. Speed" Lackhove loads "Mello Yello," mid-1990s.
Photo courtesy of John Ellsworth.

rels, and requirements that all machines have fire extinguishers and first aid kits, that anyone in the pit must wear a hardhat and eye protection, and that all machines capable of firing backward must have a backstop.

Despite all of the safety requirements and controls over how many people and who can be in the pit area of the punkin chunkin' machines, the Delaware event had its first spectator injury in 2007: a 10-year-old Lumberton, New Jersey, boy who received a concussion from a pumpkin that misfired. Association President Frank Shade said the association "didn't want a first. We definitely want him to be the last. We're going to do everything possible to make sure that doesn't happen again."

Shade said in 2008, "Our safety procedures worked. The people openly admit they were in the wrong place at the wrong time." Where 10-year-old Billy Ward and his family were was too close to a catapult owned by friends of theirs. Shade said the catapult misfired, the pumpkin went up instead of out and the family tried to scramble out of the way. The boy's mother stumbled and her fall kept her son from being able to clear the area. "Chunkers," Shade said, "know you don't run. You might be running right in the path of the pumpkin."

The young boy was a guest at the Punkin Chunkin' Association's annual banquet two weeks later and told the chunkers he was looking forward to being at the 2008 chunk.

Shade, in a 2008 interview, said the chunkers will institute further safety measures. In addition to the snow fence intended to separate the machines from the crowd and a 75-foot buffer behind the fence, Shade said the association would spend $20,000 to string 30-foot-high, half-mile long netting "like at a golf course driving range" behind the machines. He said the netting would not affect visibility but would just be another layer of safety.

CLOSE ENCOUNTERS OF THE PUMPKIN KIND

For safety reasons, punkin chunkin' machines have to be modified to meet stringent engineering standards, but the ammunition they fire – the pumpkins themselves – cannot be altered in any way. That's rule #4 in the general rules of the world championship competition. Since rule #2 for every class requires the pumpkin to leave the machine intact, the requirement that pumpkins must remain in their natural state presents a challenge and a quest for everyone trying to fling a gourd the farthest, especially since the machines themselves are hurling pumpkins at breakneck speed with tremendous force.

When Bill Thompson, Trey Melson, John Ellsworth, Don Pepper, Chuck Burton and Darryl Burton chunked their first pumpkins in 1986, the quality of the fruit wasn't much of a consideration. They only chose the first Saturday after Halloween because pumpkins would be plentiful and cheap. But pumpkin quality in the 21st century is a prime concern to anyone who doesn't want his or her pumpkin to explode in midair and become "pie in the sky."

For example, the Michigan air cannon "Second Amendment" shoots an 8-to-10-pound pumpkin from its 100-foot-long barrel at 500 miles an hour, or 733.3333 feet per second. In 2003, "Second Amendment's" second shot of the competition went 4434 feet and set a world record. That particular pumpkin, therefore, experienced the force of nearly 3.8 Gs, which is more than a Navy pilot experiences when a steam catapult launches his jet off an aircraft carrier. That's a lot of force on a gourd which usually is used to carve jack-o-lanterns or as filling for a Thanksgiving dessert.

The punkin chunkin' founding fathers may not have cared much about pumpkin quality in the beginning, but as their machines and others became more sophisticated and powerful over the years, the shape and strength of the pumpkins began to matter. In 1994 and 2002, when heavy rains left them with soft pumpkins that led to lots of pies in the sky, chunkers complained to the association about the quality of the ammunition. Though they can get their pumpkins from the association, many seek out their own from closely guard-

ABOVE: "De-Terminator's" stack of ammunition, 1995 chunk. Photo courtesy of Larry McLaughlin.

ed sources: produce stands, specific farms, or their own pumpkin patches. The World Championship Punkin Chunkin' Association website even includes a link to pumpkinnook.com, where chunkers can learn about pollination, seeds and other pumpkin-growing tips.

Some, especially the chunkers who operate air cannons and powerful centrifugal machines, have foregone the typical orange pumpkins in favor of white pumpkins. Some swear by the Lumina pumpkin, which has a lightly ribbed thicker shell that's able to withstand more force. Others, like Chuck Burton, seek out Casper pumpkins, which have a smaller hollow center and an even thicker shell. "You can throw them and they'll bounce," Burton said. "Lumina are hard but more brittle."

The search for the perfect pumpkin is never-ending and chunkers will go to almost any end to find it. "We drive up to Lancaster (Pennsylvania). New York. We have a guy near Millersville (Pennsylvania)," Burton said. "I've gone down to Virginia. North Carolina. Wherever you're going, you keep your eye out for pumpkins."

Keeping an eye out sometimes results in bringing civilians into close contact with the chunking army. Lana Browne isn't a punkin chunker. She's never been to a punkin chunkin' contest. "I can't imagine grown people throwing pumpkins." she said in a 2008 interview. But the quest for the perfect gourd brought Browne into a close encounter with one of the grown-ups who's serious about throwing pumpkins.

In the fall of 2006, Browne had a Halloween display on the porch steps of her home near Milton, Delaware. The display was traditional fall decorations: orange pumpkins, white pumpkins and chrysanthemums. She was in the house when the doorbell rang. "A man who looked like a utility company man came up in his uniform and showed me his ID," she said. She didn't remember which utility or his name, but said he told her he was there on personal business and wanted to buy the white pumpkin.

"I looked at him quizzically," she said. He asked her how much she wanted for it and she jokingly told him $500. He explained why he wanted it. "He told me he and several friends had a machine that cost $75,000, an air cannon. He said white pumpkins were difficult to find and wanted to know where we purchased it. I told him, 'a roadside stand' but couldn't remember where. He said he'd been driving up and down streets looking for white pumpkins but couldn't find any and was excited to find that pumpkin."

Browne said she "couldn't help but laugh" and told him to just take the pumpkin. But, he insisted on paying her and gave her $5 for it. She asked how he knew it was the right size. He told her he had a good eye; then, went to his truck and returned with a metal sleeve the same diameter as the barrel of his air cannon. "It was a perfect fit," Browne said. "I think punkin chunkin' is a funny thing."

AFTERWORD

Punkin chunkin,' to someone who's never done it or never seen it, as Lana Browne said, "is a funny thing." To most of those who've become involved, either as players or spectators, it's an addiction. Some have managed to get the chunkin' monkey off their backs, but for many, punkin chunkin' is something they just can't shake. .

Co-founder Bill Thompson, for example, still fires up his "Road Warrior" air cannon even though in 2007 he was out-distanced by 19 others. He's the only one of the four men recognized by the World Championship Punkin Chunkin' Association at a ceremony in 2001 as punkin chunkin's founding fathers who still is on the field. "It's fun," he said. "The inner child comes out." He also is a member of the World Championship Punkin Chunkin' Association's safety committee.

Don "Doc" Pepper, after co-founder and chunking partner John Ellsworth decided to give up chunkin' to pursue other projects, moved over to help Donny Jefferson and the centrifugal "Bad to the Bone" team. Then Pepper and Bruce Hefke dusted off Ellsworth's and Pepper's old air-powered crossbow "Under Pressure." Pepper next teamed up with Phil Norton on yet another machine, but 2007 was their last year. During the chunk, they decided it wasn't fun any more, put a "For Sale" sign on it and sold it. "I'll probably still show up on game day," Pepper said, "but I don't think I've got to run around for two months and find pumpkins and fix hydraulics."

Ellsworth stopped after the 1995 chunk. He said 10 years was enough for him; he wanted to be remembered for the ironwork he created as a blacksmith and not for building a machine that threw pumpkins. He also said punkin chunkin' began to lose its allure for him when the air cannons started showing up.

Pepper's and Ellsworth's feelings are similar to Harry "Capt. Speed" Lackhove's comment when he retired from punkin chunkin' in 1997. He told the world his "fun meter's been pegged."

Thompson's original chunkin' partner and co-founder Trey Melson launched his last pumpkin in competition in 2003. His air cannon "Universal Soldier" finished first out of 11 cannons in the adult air division that year. In 2004, he died at the age of 53. Up until his final year, his fun meter continued running, and he

An unknown punkin chunkin' machine from 1992 that probably didn't throw very far, but likely kept its creator from getting bored.
Photo courtesy of Don Pepper.

still was trying to devise the ultimate punkin chunkin' machine. His son-in-law and team member, Eric Nelson, said Melson was constantly tinkering with the idea of an electro-magnetic punkin chunkin' machine.

Melson, in more than one newspaper interview during his punkin chunkin' heyday, said he did it because it kept him from being bored.

If fending off boredom isn't enough motivation to chunk pumpkins, the quest for getting one to fly a mile surely is. Harry "Capt. Speed" Lackhove said in a 2008 interview that he will provide added incentive. To the first chunker who reaches a mile in Lackhove's lifetime, Lackhove said he will write a personal check for $1,000.

LEFT: Earliest version of "Loaded Boing," which calls itself "The World's Most Dangerous Slingshot." The early incarnation was two telephone poles stuck into the ground. A large rubber tube was stretched back 100 feet to launch pumpkins. In 1995, it launched a pumpkin 389 feet.
Photo courtesy of John Ellsworth.

RIGHT: What 10 years of dedication, punkin chunkin' addiction and tinkering can do. "Loaded Boing" in 2005, still a slingshot but with the power that year to chunk 597 feet.
Photo courtesy of Jim Riley, Team PumpkinHammer.

APPENDICES

PUNKIN CHUNKIN' BALLAD

Lyrics: Bill "Broaddog" Thompson
Music: Dawn Thompson

G   C   G
Gather around Boys, I'll tell you a story as near as I can remember,

                          D   G
It was the End of October beginning of November,

                               C   G   D   G
The air was cold and clear and I said "Boys listen Here, I Think I can make a Punkin fly."

                 C   G
John said, "Can not" I said "Can too" so we put that punkin in a bucket swung it around, away it flew. John said,

               C   G
"No Fair", I said, "Hell it's in the air".

                        C   G   D   G
So the Challenge was made and the Gauntlet was laid, to build a machine to power a punkin through the air.

                        C   G
John said, "Springs are the way to go", I said, "I don't believe so".

                            C   G   D   G
So we took some iron and steel and a frame of an automobile and we started to build a punkin chunkin' machine.

         G   C   G
Chorus: It's Punkin Chunkin' Time again come on all you neighbors and friends it's time to make them punkins

D   G   C   G   C
fly, Rain, Snow or Blow. Them Punkins are gonna go. You won't believe your eyes there goes grandma's punkin

         G   D   G
pies over Sussex County skies it's time to make them fly.

G   C   G
Well that day finally came and machines showed up from all around there were big ones, small ones, Tall ones

        D   G
and even some were upside down.

G   C   G   D   G
It was out time to play and our machines began to whale the crowd was wonderin' could they make it sail.
(Chorus)

Slow G   C   G   D
Well we won that silly bet and our friends haven't gotten over it yet and John said with a tear in his eye, "You

                               G
Country boys sure know how to make a punkin fly!" (Chorus)

WORLD CHAMPIONSHIP
PUNKIN CHUNKIN'
OFFICIAL CLASSES AND SAFETY RULES 1/6/2007 REV 8

Adult Air Class (18 and older)

1. Top machine with the longest distance wins this class. Pumpkins must weigh between 8 & 10 pounds.
2. Pumpkin must leave the machine intact.
3. No part of the machine shall cross the firing line.
4. No "wadding" (including bean chaff, straw, foam, metal, or any other object, or foreign matter).
5. No explosives are allowed! Compressed air only.
6. Pumpkin must be loaded before pressurizing tanks, and Official must see you load it
7. Pressure Air Lines must have a Check Valve near the machine end of the line.
8. A flag will be posted at the edge of the "woods" line. If a pumpkin is fired out of the field of play and into the woods, your shot will be considered a foul and you may take another shot or take measurement from the flag posted. (See General Rules number 6)
9. Only one makeup shot will be allowed per round of competition.
10. The team captain may be asked to redirect their machine. The machine will have to be reinspected after it has been redirected.
11. Horn or sound device must sound when firing downrange for safety or spotter on the field.

Adult Centrifugal Class (18 and older)

1. Pumpkins must weigh between 8 & 10 pounds.
2. Pumpkin must leave the machine intact
3. No part of the machine shall cross the firing line.
4. No "wadding" (including bean chaff, straw, foam, metal, or any other object, or foreign matter)
5. Machines shall spin at least 1 revolution before chunkin'.
6. These machines require Backstops.
7. A flag will be posted at the edge of the "woods" line. If a pumpkin is fired out of the field of play and into the woods, your shot will be considered a foul and you may take another shot or take measurement from the flag posted. (See General Rules number 6)
8. Note: Centrifugal machines are any machines that spin the pumpkin more than 1 full revolution.
9. Only one makeup shot will be allowed per round of competition.
10. The team captain may be asked to redirect their machine.
11. The machine will have to be reinspected after it has been redirected.

Adult Catapult Class (18 and older)

1. Pumpkins must weigh between 8 & 10 pounds
2. . Pumpkin must leave the machine intact.
3. No part of the machine shall cross the firing line.
4. No "wadding" (including bean chaff, straw, foam, metal, or any other object, or foreign matter).
5. Machine shall consist of springs, cords, rubber, dead weights, or other mechanical means of creating stored energy.
6. Motorized winches and/or other cranking devices may cock the machine.

7. These Machines require Backstops

8. A flag will be posted at the edge of the "woods" line. If a pumpkin is fired out of the field of play and into the woods, your shot will be considered a foul and you may take another shot or take measurement from the flag posted. (See General Rules number 6)

9. Only one makeup shot will be allowed per round of competition.

10. The team captain may be asked to redirect their machine. The machine will have to be reinspected after it has been redirected.

11. Horn or sound device must sound when firing downrange for safety or spotter on the field.

Adult Trebuchet Class (18 and older)

1. Pumpkins must weigh between 8 & 10 pounds.

2. Pumpkin must leave the machine intact.

3. No part of the machine shall cross the firing line.

4. No "wadding" (including bean chaff, straw, foam, meal, or any other object, or foreign matter).

5. Machine shall consist of swinging, or fixed counterweights. They can be made of wood, metal, or plastic.

6. Motorized winches and/or other cranking devices may cock the machine

7. These Machines require Backstops

8. A flag will be posted at the edge of the "woods" line. If a pumpkin is fired out of the field of play and into the woods, your shot will be considered a foul and you may take another shot or take measurement from the flag posted. (See General Rules number 6)

9. Only one makeup shot will be allowed per round of competition.

10. The team captain may be asked to redirect their machine. The machine will have to be reinspected after it has been redirected.

11. Horn or sound device must sound when firing downrange for safety or spotter on the field.

Adult Human Power Class (18 and older)

1. Pumpkins must weigh between 8 & 10 pounds.

2. Pumpkin must leave the machine intact.

3. No part of the machine shall cross the firing line

4. No "wadding" (including bean chaff, straw, foam, metal, or any other object, or foreign matter).

5. Machines can use any kind of stored energy that can be stored by a single person in two minutes. (Energy must be stored by the power of this one person, not by other means.)

6. Contestants shall be given a maximum of (2) two minutes from the start of cocking their machine until fully cocked and locked for safety. (This does not include the three (3) minute rule for being ready to fire).

7. Some may require Backstops due to the type of machine.

8. A flag will be posted at the edge of the "woods" line. If a pumpkin is fired out of the field of play and into the woods, your shot will be considered a foul and you may take another shot or take measurement from the flag posted. (See General Rules number 6.)

9. Horn or sound device must sound when firing downrange for safety of spotter on the field.

Note: Human power machines will be allowed time to cock plus time to secure and fire. The cocking time will be limited to 2 minutes. Secure and fire time is (3) minutes like all machines.

Adult Human Power Centrifugal Class (18 and older)

1. Pumpkins must weigh between 8 & 10 pounds.

2. Pumpkin must leave the machine intact.

3. No part of the machine shall cross the firing line.

4. No "wadding" (including bean chaff, straw, foam, metal, or any other object, or foreign matter)

5. Machines can use any kind of stored energy that can be stored by a single person in two minutes. (Energy must be stored by the power of this one person, not by other means.)

6. Contestants shall be given a maximum of (2) two minutes from the start of cocking their machine until fully cocked and locked for safety. (This does not include the three (3) minute rule for being ready to fire)

7. These machines require Backstops

8. A flag will be posted at the edge of the "woods" line. If a pumpkin is fired out of the field of play and into the woods, your shot will be considered a foul and you may take another shot or take measurement from the flag posted. (See General Rules number 6.)

9. Note: Centrifugal machines are any machines that spin the pumpkin more than 1 full revolution. Note: Human power machines will be allowed time to cock plus time to secure and fire. The cocking time will be limited to 2 minutes. Secure and fire time is (3) minutes like all machines.

10. Horn or sound device must sound when firing downrange for safety of spotter on the field.

Adult Torsion Catapult Class (18 and older)

1. Pumpkins must weigh between 8 & 10 pounds.

2. Pumpkin must leave the machine intact.

3. No part of the machine shall cross the firing line.

4. No "wadding" (including bean chaff, straw, foam, metal, or any other object, or foreign matter).

5. Machine shall consist of torsion springs, or cords that once wrapped around its axle (pivot point) will create a stored energy.

6. Motorized winches and/or other cranking devices may cock the machine.

7. These Machines require Backstops

8. A flag will be posted at the edge of the "woods" line. If a pumpkin is fired out of the field of play and into the woods, your shot will be considered a foul and you may take another shot or take measurement from the flag posted. (See General Rules number 6)

9. Only one makeup shot will be allowed per round of competition.

10. The team captain may be asked to redirect their machine. The machine will have to be reinspected after it has been redirected.

11. Horn or sound device must sound when firing downrange for safety or spotter on the field.

Theatrical Class

1. Pumpkins can weigh anything you want them to weigh.

2. Pumpkin must leave the machine intact. (To stay with the theme)

3. No part of the machine shall cross the firing line.

Wadding sounds like fun for this class. Must look great... (You are responsible for cleanup)

3. No age limit.

5. Machines limited to chunkin' 100' or less. (Distance is not the goal; ability to ham it up is the goal).

6. Teams will be judged on the show, each team can hold as many shows per day that they wish to perform.

7. The selected PCA judges will set judging times.

8. Horn or sound device must sound when firing downrange for the safety of the spotter on the field.

9. Cannon machine or throwing device on theatrical division must have an inspection.

Youth 11-17 Air Class

1. Pumpkins must weigh no less than 4 lbs.
2. Pumpkin must leave the machine intact
3. No part of the machine shall cross the firing line
4. No "wadding" (including bean chaff, straw, foam, metal, or any other object, or foreign matter).
5. No explosives are allowed! Compressed air only.
6. Machines must have adult supervision on the design and building.
7. Machines must be assembled, loaded, and chunked by children of the proper age group under full adult supervision.
8. Pumpkin must be loaded before pressurizing tanks, and Official must see you load it.
9. Pressure airline needs a check valve near the machine end.
10. A flag will be posted at the edge of the "woods" line. If a pumpkin is fired out of the field of play and into the woods, your shot will be considered a foul and you may take another shot or take measurement from the flag posted. (See General Rules number 6)
11. Only one makeup shot will be allowed per round of competition.
12. The team captain may be asked to redirect their machine. The machine will have to be reinspected after it has been redirected.
13. Children or youth in pits must be under adult supervision at all times. Example: Youth could fire machine while unattended and be injured or injure someone else.
14. Horn or sound device must sound when firing downrange for the safety of the spotter on the field.

Youth 11-17 Catapult Class

1. Pumpkins must weigh no less than 4 pounds.
2. Pumpkin must leave the machine intact.
3. No part of the machine shall cross the firing line
4. No "wadding" (including bean chaff, straw, foam, metal, or any other object, or foreign matter)
5. Machine shall consist of springs, cords, rubber, dead weights, or other mechanical means of creating a stored energy
6. Motorized winches and/or other cranking devices may cock the machine.
7. Machines must have adult supervision on the design and building.
8. Machines must be assembled, loaded, and chunked by children of the proper age group under full adult supervision.
9. These machines need a Backstop
10. A flag will be posted at the edge of the "woods" line. If a pumpkin is fired out of the field of play and into the woods, your shot will be considered a foul and you may take another shot or take measurement from the flag posted. (See General Rules number 6)
11. Only one makeup shot will be allowed per round of competition.
12. The team captain may be asked to redirect their machine. The machine will have to be reinspected after it has been redirected.
13. Children or youth in pits must be under adult supervision at all times. Example: Youth could fire machine while unattended and be injured or injure someone else.
14. Horn or sound device must sound when firing downrange for the safety of the spotter on the field.

Youth 11-17 Trebuchet Class

1. Pumpkins must weigh no less than 4 pounds
2. Pumpkin must leave the machine intact.

3. No part of the machine shall cross the firing line.

4. No "wadding" (including bean chaff, straw, foam, metal, or any other object, or foreign matter).

5. Machine shall consist of swinging, or fixed counterweights. They can be made of wood, metal, or plastic.

6. Machines must have adult supervision on the design and building.

7. Machines must be assembled, loaded, and fired by children of the proper age group under full adult supervision

8. Motorized winches and/or other cranking devices may cock the machine.

9. These Machines require Backstops.

10. A flag will be posted at the edge of the "woods" line. If a pumpkin is fired out of the field of play and into the woods, your shot will be considered a foul and you may take another shot or take measurement from the flag posted. (See General Rules number 6)

11. Only one makeup shot will be allowed per round of competition.

12. The team captain may be asked to redirect their machine. The machine will have to be reinspected after it has been redirected.

13. Children or youth in pits must be under adult supervision at all times. Example: Youth could fire machine while unattended and be injured or injure someone else.

14. Horn or sound device must sound when firing downrange for the safety of the spotter on the field.

Youth 11-17 Human Power Class

1. Pumpkins must weigh no less than 4 pounds.

2. Pumpkin must leave the machine intact.

3. No part of the machine shall cross the firing line.

4. No "wadding" (including bean chaff, straw, foam, metal, or any other object, or foreign matter)

5. Machines can use any kind of stored energy that can be stored by a single person in two minutes. (Energy must be stored by the power of this one person, not by other means.)

6. Contestants shall be given a maximum of (2) two minutes from the start of cocking their machine until fully cocked and locked for safety. (This does not include the three (3) minute rule for being ready to fire)

7. Machines must have adult supervision on the design and building.

8. Machines must be assembled, loaded, and fired by children of the proper age group under full adult supervision.

9. Some may require Backstops due to the type of machine.

Note: Human power machines will be allowed the time to cock plus time to secure and fire. The cocking time will be limited to 2 minutes. Secure and fire time is three (3) minutes like all machines.

10. Only one makeup shot will be allowed per round of competition.

11. The team captain may be asked to redirect their machine. The machine will have to be reinspected after it has been redirected.

12. Children or youth in pits must be under adult supervision at all times. Example: Youth could fire machine while unattended and be injured or injure someone else.

13. Horn or sound device must sound when firing downrange for the safety of the spotter on the field.

Youth 10-Under Catapult Class

1. Pumpkins must weigh no less than 2 pounds.

2. Pumpkin must leave the machine intact

3. No part of the machine shall cross the firing line.

4. No "wadding" (including bean chaff, straw, foam, metal, or any other object, or foreign matter).

5. Machine shall consist of springs, cords, rubber, dead weights, or other mechanical means of creating a stored energy.

6. Motorized winches and/or other cranking devices may cock the machine.

7. Machines must have adult supervision on the design and building.

8. Machines are expected to be set up and fired under full adult supervision.

9. These Machines need a Backstop.

10. A flag will be posted at the edge of the "woods" line. If a pumpkin is fired out of the field of play and into the woods, your shot will be considered a foul and you may take another shot or take measurement from the flag posted. (See General Rules number 6)

11. Only one makeup shot will be allowed per round of competition.

12. The team captain may be asked to redirect their machine. The machine will have to be reinspected after it has been redirected.

13. Children or youth in pits must be under adult supervision at all times. Example: Youth could fire machine while unattended and be injured or injure someone else.

14. Horn or sound device must sound when firing downrange for the safety of the spotter on field of competition.

Youth 10-Under Trebuchet Class

1. Pumpkins must weigh no less than 2 pounds.

2. Pumpkin must leave the machine intact.

3. No part of the machine shall cross the firing line.

4. No "wadding" (including bean chaff, straw, foam, metal, or any other object, or foreign matter).

5. Machine shall consist of swinging, or fixed counterweights. They can be made of wood, metal, or plastic.

6. Machines must have adult supervision on the design and building.

7. Machines are expected to be set up and fired under full adult supervision

8. Motorized winches and/ or other cranking devices may cock the machine.

9. These Machines require Backstops.

10. A flag will be posted at the edge of the "woods" line. If a pumpkin is fired out of the field of play and into the woods, your shot will be considered a foul and you may take another shot or take measurement from the flag posted. (See General Rules number 6)

11. Only one makeup shot will be allowed per round of competition.

12. The team captain may be asked to redirect their machine. The machine will have to be reinspected after it has been redirected.

13. Children or youth in pits must be under adult supervision at all times. Example: Youth could fire machine while unattended and be injured or injure someone else.

14. Horn or sound device must sound when firing downrange for the safety of the spotter on the field.

Youth 10-Under Human Power Class

1. Pumpkins must weigh no less than 2 pounds.

2. Pumpkin must leave the machine intact.

3. No part of the machine shall cross the firing line.

4. No "wadding" (including bean chaff, straw, foam, metal, or any other object, or foreign matter).

5. Machines can use any kind of energy that can be stored by a single person in two minutes. (Energy must be stored by the power of this one person, not by other means.)

6. Contestants shall be given a maximum of (2) two minutes from the start of cocking their machine until fully cocked and locked for safety. (This does not include the three (3) minute rule for being ready to fire).

7. Machines must have adult supervision on the design and building.

8. Machines are expected to be set up and fired under full adult supervision.

9. Some may require Backstops due to the type of machine.

Note: Human power machines will be allowed the time to cock plus time to secure and fired. The cocking time will be limited to 2 minutes. Secure and fire time is three (3) minutes like all machines.

10. Only one makeup shot will be allowed per round of competition.

11. The team captain may be asked to redirect their machine.

12. The machine will have to be reinspected after it has been redirected.

13. Horn or sound device must sound when firing downrange for the safety of the spotter on the field.

14. Children or youth in pits must be under adult supervision at all times. Example: Youth could fire machine while unattended and be injured or injure someone else.

General Rules

1. The World Championship Punkin Chunkin' Association reserves the right to combine any classes if there is a lack of participation. Any class that is subject to cutting will be contacted to see where they want to be moved. This will mean they must meet the full qualifications of the class they move to. All classes must have Three (3) entries in that class to open it to competition. If any Class is cut for the year it will need 3 entries to open it again in the future.

2. Machines can only enter one (1) class per machine. Teams entering two machines on the same trailer in the same class may do so, provided they do not share components and they pay for both entries.

3. All Machines must be able to fire within three (3) minutes. Human power will get an additional two (2) minutes to cock the machine. (Keep in mind that every attempt is made to give you (20) minutes by informing you 4 machines or more down the firing line.) Any machine not able to fire when the pit boss decides your three (3) minutes are up will forfeit that round. NO EXCEPTIONS! Team captains are responsible for making sure they get their pumpkin weighed well enough in advance to ensure they have the time they need to set up. Any special needs or concessions about time needed for your machine should be brought up at the team captains' meeting. The PCA and Pit Boss will try to work with you to ensure you the notice you need. Again, Team Captains are responsible for making sure you're ready when it's your turn to chunk.

4. Pumpkins are not to be altered in any way, excluding PCA marker paints. All pumpkins must be in their natural state. Pumpkins fired from machine during competition will be measured from the front of or the farthest point of machine. Your pit number may be written on your pumpkin to help in the identification at the landing zone.

5. All machines must be set up in the assigned areas. You will be given notice of this area well in advance. No excuses will be entertained for not being in your spot (on game day). You will be required to move.

6. A flag will be posted at the edge of the "woods" line. If a pumpkin is fired out of the field of play and into the woods, your shot will be considered a foul and you may take another shot or take measurement from the flag posted. Only one makeup shot will be allowed per round of competition. The team captain may be asked to redirect their machine. The machine will have to be reinspected after it has been redirected by the safety instructor.

7. When using an 8-10 lb. pumpkin, the longest distance of the event is the WORLD CHAMPION PUNKIN CHUNKER and wins the overall chunk regardless of class. All other first-place winners are Champions of class entered.

8. Any machine using compressed air must have the pumpkin loaded before pressure is developed.

9. The pit boss starts the three (3) hour clock (logged) for the team taking option to have spotters locate pumpkin. If any captain should request a log report for a competitive team this will be made available to him/her (Please see pit boss)

10. It is the responsibility of the prior year's champion to return the traveling trophy to the current year's World Championships in DE. The trophy must be kept in good condition.

11. If you are disqualified for any round in competition for breaking SAFETY or REGULAR rules you will forfeit your longest distance, not the distance of the shot you are being disqualified on.

12. All machines and equipment used by chunkers must be removed from the field within two weeks after the Punkin Chunkin' Competition. Owner or team captain will pay towing and storage expenses for machine and equipment left on field after deadline. Children or youth in pits must be under adult supervision at all times. Example: youth could fire machine while unattended and be injured or injure someone else.

Safety Rules

1. Hoses must be in good operating condition. Chafed or cut hoses must not be used. If using Chicago-type quick connects, safety pins must be installed in each of the two holes. Any manufacturer- recommended safety equipment designed for any type of coupler must be used. All air lines 1" in diameter and larger must be cabled to a stationary device.

2. Make sure all sections of your cannon barrel are properly secured so that they will not separate and will stay stationary. Make sure you do not pinch or collapse your barrel when using aluminum barrel. All cannons not using an actuated valve powered by air or some other mechanical device must have a spring loaded normally open valve. The use of Plastic Polyvinyl Chloride (PVC) will not be allowed for the use of air cannon barrels in the fire line up, due to the safety hazard of this type of pipe. This pipe is for the use of liquids, not compressed air. The manufacturer of the pipe states it is unsafe to transport air in PVC pipe no matter what schedule you use. Air tanks made of PVC will be illegal. No PVC or plastic is allowed in pressurized areas.

3. Aluminum barrels suspended by cables must have the cables anchored to a substantial base to prevent whipping around. Plastic coated cable will not be allowed

4. All machine captains and teammates are to follow World Championship Punkin Chunkin' Association Rules or you will be penalized or disqualified, depending on the nature of which rule is broken. If you are penalized, you will forfeit your chance to chunk in that round of competition. If disqualified, you will be referred to rule #11 of the General Rules. Major infractions that are deemed as challenging the safety of the chunk and/or others around your machine will be discussed during a quorum of PCA trustees and Safety Committee to decide on the actions to take. The results of the Quorum will be relayed to the team captain. There will be ZERO TOLERANCE for those who break safety rules.

5. The WCPCA reserves the right to request a team captain to dismantle his or her machine to inspect for foul play. For example, use of any other propellant other than compressed air. If you are caught using any chemicals (NITROGEN, HELIUM, HYDROGEN, or any illegal substances other than compressed air) you will be banned from The World Championship Punkin Chunkin'.

6. All portable air storage vessels used to fill their cannon must be stood upright and secured to a stationary device. No tanks or vessels may be stored lying down on the ground or transported ly-

ing down in any vehicle. Every vessel must have a safety cap on it when not in use. All nipples, fittings, manifolds, or airlines must be capable of handling the pressure of air on them. This is your responsibility. All propane tanks must be secured to a stationary device.

7. All catapult and trebuchet machines must have a safety strap or mechanism to hold the throwing arm or boom in case of early fire when loading. You are responsible for making sure everyone stays clear behind your machine, in case of a misfire. Personnel handling ropes or cable should wear gloves such as a sailing or repelling type to prevent burns. Teams are recommended to use a safety harness when climbing over 10 feet high of the ground.

8. Inspect all hydraulic lines each time you cock or lift your machine. Make sure winches can handle the load and cables are in good condition. Make sure your release mechanisms are heavy enough to handle the load. Make sure you have an automatic brake or a dog lock on winch or cocking device. Tie-downs on cannons should not be directly to the barrel. All cannons must be secured to prevent upward recoil. It is the machine designer's responsibility to make sure winch and cables can handle the load put on them. Also, cables and clamps must be installed correctly. Cannons, machines or throwing devices on theatrical division must be inspected.

9. NO CHILDREN under 16 will be allowed to drive golf carts, four-wheelers, dirt bikes, or ATVs alone. They may ride with an adult that has a valid driver's license. All golf carts, four-wheelers, dirt bikes or ATVs must display their pit number on that vehicle in clear view. The DELAWARE STATE POLICE on the chunkin' field may control the use of this type of vehicle. No golf carts, four- wheelers, dirt bikes, or ATVs, are permitted on the field beyond firing line unless you are an association official or spotter actively engaged in spotting pumpkins.

10. Only 1 Team spotter will be allowed on field per team and must remain out there until released. Also he must sign in & out at security tent. All spotters on motorized vehicles will operate their vehicles AT THEIR OWN RISK!

11. Backstops will be required for any machine that can fire backwards (even if it never has done so). The WCPCA will provide backstops for teams to share (take turns firing). Teams may make their own stops for the chunk but they must be constructed to a WCPCA approved design standard. (Standard attached) Any machine inspected on the field or approved in advance, as "not able to fire backwards" will be exempt from this requirement. Machines marked for backstops that fire without one will be disqualified from the chunk. This includes anytime they fire while on the field

12. . Any machine found to have structural defects (weld fractures affecting the pressure vessel, load beams, firing pins, any load bearing members, supports or support subsystems) will be banned from chunking until repaired and re-inspected by a member of the safety committee.

13. Safety committee end-of-day meeting – The safety committee will have approximately a 4 p.m. meeting each day if there are safety issues present. We welcome team captains to do so at this time. Note: No inspections after dark. No pets allowed in pits.

14. All team captains must sign the field roster stating that they have received, read, and understand the rules of the World Championship Punkin Chunkin' Association. This sheet will be on the field and given to the pit boss. If it is not signed, you do not chunk. All team captains must attend all safety field meetings. If the daily meeting roster is not signed at the end of the morning meeting, you will not be tracked down and the team will not compete that day of competition.

15. Compressed air machines must have a bleed-off device (valve) to allow for safely removing the air if the machine cannot be fired. This device should be installed such that it does not blow directly to the dirt or face level to prevent Eye injury. If it is exposed to the body level it should have a shield installed to deflect the air. Air Lines must have a Check Valve near the machine end of line. Ceasefire: no machine is to fire when a ceasefire has been ordered. If you locked and loaded or pressurized at this

time, contact security/pit boss/safety committee so you can safely discharge or bleed off air pressure. Pop-off relief safety valves must have plastic shipping plugs removed when pressurizing any cannon or machine. Pop-off relief valves are not to be altered or held down to prevent popping off. Pop-off relief valves are not to be reclosed after opening on their own while machine is being pressurized to fire.

16. Machines may not chunk until the safety committee inspects and approves them to be safe by the WORLD CHAMPIONSHIP PUNKIN CHUNKIN' SAFETY RULES. Any alterations after being inspected will require another inspection to be able to fire. If your machine has been inspected, you will need to be reinspected by a safety inspector official in order to fire again. The safety committee may require the team captain to fire their machine during the inspection process to ensure the machine is safe enough to compete at the World Championship Chunk.

17. Hard Hats and Eye Protection to be worn by all fire line personnel in pit when firing

18. Each Machine must have a Fire Extinguisher mounted to the machine and a First Aid Kit in plain view and clearly marked for all people to see, but not on the machine

19. The following rules are State of Delaware requirements enforced by the Department of Natural Resources and Environmental Control (DNREC). They are non-negotiable.

    1. All pressure vessels shall be built to the American Society of Mechanical Engineers (A.S.M.E.) construction codes. The vessels will have a manufacturer's nameplate with proper (A.S.M.E.) stamping and will be marked with the vessel's allowable working pressure.

    2. All pressure vessels shall be equipped with an A.S.M.E. approved and scaled relief valve set at or below the allowable working pressure of the vessel. A smaller A.S.M.E. relief valve can be placed on the vessel when the operation requires the tank to be filled from a cylinder tank. This valve will be set at or below the allowable working pressure of the vessel. All relief valves must be maintained in proper working order during operation of the vessel. The relief valve will need approval by the boiler safety division, so it is recommended you contact them before purchasing the valve.

    3. Each vessel shall be inspected by the Delaware Division of Boilers safety and issued an operating certificate. These certificates are valid for four years from the date of inspection/issuance. This certificate must be in hand before the machine can enter the field.

    4. Each vessel shall have a hydrostatic test conducted in accordance with the test procedures in the national board inspection code. Each vessel must be hydrostatically tested every two years and witnessed by a National Board Commissioned inspector and the results recorded and presented at time of inspection by the department. If a third party National Board Commissioned inspector is not used, a department inspector can witness the test on any vessel upon request. If out-of-state vessels are to be inspected by a department inspector the vessel must be in Delaware no later then Wednesday before the event.

    5. A.S.M.E. vessels now in operation are considered grandfathered under these conditions. Any future alterations and repairs made to the pressure vessel must meet the National Board of Boilers and pressure vessel Inspectors Code (NBBIC). Any air cannons constructed after the 2004 event must meet existing Department regulations and the vessel must be mounted in a cradle type mount with no welding of the vessel to the frame.

    6. All vessels regardless of origination, operated at the event must meet these requirements.

    7. The World Championship Punkin Chunkin' Association is not in a position to deviate from the Department of Natural Resources and Environmental requirements and must ensure enforcement of those requirements.

WORLD CHAMPIONSHIP PUNKIN CHUNKIN' RECORDS

Class	Team	Home	Distance (in feet)	Year
Adult Air	Second Amendment	MI	4434.28	2003
Adult Centrifugal	Bad to the Bone	DE	2770.74	2004
Adult Catapult	Fibonacci Unlimited II	MA	2862.28	2005
Adult Trebuchet	Yankee Siege	NH	1702.46	2005
Adult Human Powered	Gene's Machine	DE	1827.57	2004
Adult Torsion	Chucky II	NJ	2020.76	2006
Adult Centrifugal Human Powered	M2S2 Spinumpkin	PA	229.59	2005
Youth Air	Young Glory III	DE	3945.28	2003
Youth Catapult	Little Feats	MD	1232.94	2005
Youth Trebuchet	Pumpkin Whipper	CT	749.00	2005
Youth Human Powered	Failed Negotiations	IL	853.46	2006
Youth 10 & Under	Little Blaster	DE	1939.81	2002

Source: World Championship Punkin Chunkin' Association

RECORD YOUR OWN WORLD CHAMPIONSHIP PUNKIN CHUNKIN' RECORDS

Class	Team	Home	Distance (in feet)	Year
Adult Air				
Adult Centrifugal				
Adult Catapult				
Adult Trebuchet				
Adult Human Powered				
Adult Torsion				
Adult Centrifugal Human Powered				
Youth Air				
Youth Catapult				
Youth Trebuchet				
Youth Human Powered				
Youth 10 & Under				

YEAR-BY-YEAR RESULTS FOR WORLD CHAMPIONSHIP PUNKIN CHUNKIN'
(Longest Chunk by Team; 1st, 2nd & 3rd Place Only)

Year	Class	Team	Distance (feet)
1986	No classes	Trey Melson & Bill Thompson Chuck & Darryl Burton John Ellsworth & Don Pepper	*178 150 or so 70 or so
1987	No classes	Trey Melson & Bill Thompson John Ellsworth & Don Pepper Larry McLaughlin	496 197 or 210 156
1988	No classes		All the pumpkins landed in the woods. Everyone claims to be the winner.
1989	Unlimited	One-Eyed Jack (John Ellsworth) Mello Yello III	612.00 225.08
	Catapult	Mishaps	114.50
1990	Classes aren't clear.	Ultimate Warrior Flipper Mean Green Pumpkin Machine	776.00 593.00 ***398.00
1991	Unlimited	Ultimate Warrior Mello Yello Flipper	607.50 575.00 436.50
	Youth	Lean Mean Catapulting Team	91.00
1992	Unlimited	De-Terminator Ultimate Warrior	852.00 800 plus
	(Incomplete records)		
1993	Unlimited	Under Pressure De-Terminator Ultimate Warrior	1024.00 826.00 803.00
	Human Powered	Sussex Tech Engineers	92.16
	Youth 10 and Under	Ejackolantern Punkin Masters	128.16
	Youth 11-17	Teen Terminators (Cape Henlopen HS)	202.00
1994	Unlimited	Universal Soldier Under Pressure Bad to the Bone	2508.00 1303.00 1132.00

Year	Class	Team	Distance (feet)
1994 (continued)	Human Powered	Hawks	246.20
		Gene's Machine	85.40
		Punkin Thruster	78.40
	Youth 10 and under	Binoculars Required	68.10
		Overbrook Sling Shooters	49.50
		Roadrunner Special	26.50
	Youth 11 - 17	Sussex Tech	67.70
		The Wolverine Bandit	62.40
		Good Shepherd Youth Group	36.10
1995	Unlimited Air Cannon	Mello Yello	2655.00
		Universal Soldier	2240.00
		Top Secret	1647.00
	Unlimited Centrifugal	De-Terminator	1592.00
		Bad to the Bone	1226.00
		Blowin' Chunks	150.00
	Unlimited Catapult	Under Pressure	1504.00
		Loaded Boing	389.00
		Sudden Impact	60.00
	Human Powered	Gene's Machine	526.00
		Jay Iceman's Blue Hen Hurler (U of D)	398.00
		Bruce Hefke's Hercules	279.00
	Youth 10 and under	Calculatin' Cubs of Pack 944	76.00
	Youth 11 - 17	Binoculars Required	144.00
		Caesar Rodney Tech Education Team	86.00
		Apostolic Assault	41.00
1996**	Air Cannon	Aludium Q36 Pumpkin Modulator	2710.00
		Mello Yello	2629.00
		Old Glory	2269.00
	Centrifugal	Bad to the Bone	1675.00
		De-Terminator	1252.00
		Ultimate Warrior	830.00
	Catapult	Loaded Boing	493.00
	Human Powered	Gene's Machine	576.00
		Adam's Packer	412.00
		Onager	398.00
	Youth 11-17	DelCastle Tech	759.00
		Sussex Tech	172.00
		Caesar Rodney HS	162.00
	Youth 10 & Under	Calculatin' Catapultin' Cubs of Pack 994	118
1997	Air Cannon	Universal Soldier	3718.00
		Aludium Q36 Pumpkin Modulator	3541.00
		Old Glory	3146.00

Year	Class	Team	Distance (feet)
1997 (continued)	Centrifugal	Bad to the Bone Ultimate Warrior De-Terminator	2008.00 1568.00 1188.00
	Catapult	Gene's Machine	1105.00
	Human Powered	Gene's Machine Onager Adam's Packer	866.00 581.00 545.00
	Youth 12-17	Spirit of the Cougar Blue Heron	1192.00 442.00
	Youth 11 & Under	Young Glory Miscalculation	630.00 135.00
1998	Pneumatic	Aludium Q36 Pumpkin Modulator Old Glory Universal Soldier	4026.32 3407.62 3100.50
	Adult Unlimited	Gene's Machine Jack-O-Launcher Loaded Boing	1214.62 742.66 712.00
	Adult Centrifugal	Bad to the Bone Ultimate Warrior De-Terminator	2107.00 1460.62 1390.94
	Adult Human Powered	Gene's Machine Onager Manual Lobber	1194.76 793.72 831.42
	Youth Unlimited	Young Glory Spirit of the Cougar	863.50 477.24
	Youth 11-17	Jack-O-Launcher Free Delivery Miscalculation	647.82 233.00 159.70
	Youth 10 & Under	Go Away Young Punkin	197.30
1999	Air Cannon	Big Ten Inch Aludium Q36 Pumpkin Modulator Old Glory	3694.60 3539.00 3404.46
	Centrifugal	Bad to the Bone De-Terminator Fibonacci	1958.00 1433.88 1383.44
	Catapult	Gene's Machine Hypertension Feats Don't Fail Me Now	1647.56 950.00 745.22
	Human Powered	Gene's Machine Onager Pumpkin Slayer	1327.98 1119.00 1095.74
	Human Powered	Gene's Machine Onager Pumpkin Slayer	1327.98 1119.00 1095.74

Year	Class	Team	Distance (feet)
1999 (continued)	Youth Unlimited	Young Glory	2320.11
		Pumpkin Eater	2150.54
		Pumpkinator	1934.11
	Youth	Free Delivery	623.02
		Perpetual Velocity	614.69
		42 Buckmaster	253.12
2000	Air Cannon	Old Glory	4085.00
		Aludium Q36 Pumpkin Modulator	3860.00
		2nd Amendment	3632.98
	Centrifugal	Bad to the Bone	2127.63
		De-Terminator	160.70
	Catapult	Acme Catapult Co.	1603.31
		Hypertension	1361.07
		Gene's Machine	1276.02
	Trebuchet	Prince Valiant	458.49
		Junk Yard Chunker	435.61
		Dels Destroyer	396.96
	Human Powered	Acme Spookey Bazookey	1334.84
		Gene's Machine	1318.36
		Hypertension	1122.99
	Youth Unlimited	Free Delivery	775.32
		Gourd Slinger	526.96
		Big Bruin	369.10
	Youth 10 & Under	Little Feats	707.16
		Chapel School	70.03
2001**	Air Cannon	Old Glory	3911.02
		Universal Soldier	3718.77
		2nd Amendment	3649.29
	Centrifugal	Bad to the Bone	2134.20
		De-Terminator	1114.05
	Catapult	Hypertension	1578.20
		Pumpkin Slayer	1408.91
		Fibonacci-140	1244.76
	Trebuchet	King Arthur	643.69
		Punkin Air	614.58
		Regulator	603.06
	Human Powered	Gene's Machine	1418.32
		Onager	1145.16
		Destrien	750.46
	Youth Unlimited	Young Glory III	3229.26
		Punkin Eater	3184.43
		Punkinator	2500.36
	Youth 11-17	Free Delivery	693.44
		Little Feats	676.55
		Bandit	367.04

Year	Class	Team	Distance (feet)
2001 (continued)	Youth 10 & Under	Pomeroy Sister Slinger	260.50
		Lunch Launcher	67.71
	Theatrical	Pirates O' the Chunk	2.00
2002**	Air Cannon	2nd Amendment	3881.54
		Big Ten Inch	3816.64
		Universal Soldie	3631.78
	Centrifugal	Bad to the Bone	2358.62
		De-Terminator	1087.69
		Southern Exposure	105.69
	Catapult	Hypertension	1728.34
		Acme Catapult	1710.40
		Feats Don't Fail Me Now	1138.38
	Trebuchet	King Arthur	927.17
		Regulator	804.76
		PumpkinHammer	717.21
	Human Powered	Gene's Machine	1507.55
		Punkin Slayer	1383.60
		Onager	1157.79
	Youth Unlimited	Gourd Thrasher	3019.96
		Young Glory III	2922.99
		Punkin Eater	2700.23
	Youth 11-17	Little Feats	808.84
		Subjugator 3	437.06
		Pumpkin Beyond	379.16
	Youth 10 & Under	Little Blaster	1939.81
		Pomeroy Sister Slinger	449.36
		Pomeroy Hurler	62.12
2003**	Championship Air Cannon	2nd Amendment	4434.28
		Old Glory	3665.89
		Big Ten Inch	3591.16
	Adult Air Cannon	Universal Soldier	3473.25
		Grand Emancipator	3420.07
		Fire & Ice	3363.84
	Adult Centrifugal	Bad to the Bone	2341.70
		De-Terminator	1116.76
		M2S2 Spinumpkin	133.84
	Adult Catapult	Fibonacci	****1752.81
		Acme Catapult	1752.81
		Hypertension	1586.00
	Adult Trebuchet	King Arthur	1150.34
		PumpkinHammer	1024.78
		Regulator	894.84
	Adult Human Powered	Gene's Machine	1730.61
		Splat Cat	692.56
		Punkin Up Chunkin'	470.37

Year	Class	Team	Distance (feet)
2003 (continued)	Adult Torsion	Onager	1341.15
		Chucky	848.44
		Mista Ballista	290.96
	Youth 11-17 Air Cannon	Young Glory III	3945.28
		Gourd Thrasher	3586.52
		Punkinator	3118.99
	Youth 11-17 Catapult	Little Feats	801.85
		Rock Howitzer	427.90
		G-Uni	256.8
	Youth 11-17 Trebuchet	Burning Daylight	161.63
		Mighty Mighty Mariner	147.68
		Grendel	119.59
	Youth 10 & Under	Sister Slinger	526.97
		Jersey Devil	362.94
		Shelltown Man	65.40
2004**	Adult Air Cannon	Old Glory	4224.00
		2nd Amendment	4065.60
		Fire & Ice	3970.00
	Adult Centrifugal	Bad to the Bone	2770.74
		De-Terminator	45.00
	Adult Catapult	Hypertension	2111.58
		Fibonacci	2090.73
		Feats Don't Fail Me Now	1876.22
	Adult Trebuchet	Yankee Siege	1394.29
		PumpkinHammer	1350.74
		King Arthur	1133.29
	Adult Human Powered	Gene's Machine	1827.57
		Pumpkin Slayer	1357.48
		Destrier	931.25
	Adult Torsion	Onager	1504.62
		Chucky II	1326.20
		Mista Ballista	358.73
	Adult Centrifugal Human Powered	Pumpkin Putter	176.84
		Spinning Wheel Chunker	160.47
		M2S2 Spinumpkin	120.77
	Youth 11-17 Air Cannon	Young Glory III	3643.72
		Punkinator	3343.67
		Gourd Thrasher	3265.14
	Youth 11-17 Catapult	Little Feats	558.49
		Bandit	327.35
		Brothers in Arm	140.75
	Youth 11-17 Trebuchet	Pumpkin Whipper	397.78
		Aeron	390.73
		New Subjugato	368.74

Year	Class	Team	Distance (feet)
2004 (continued)	Youth 10 & Under	Sister Slinger	505.99
		Little Miss Liberty/Julia's Machine	268.33
		Shelltown Man	44.77
	Theatrical	Pirates of Punkin Chunkin'	
		Boing 30	
2005**	Adult Air Cannon	2nd Amendment	4331.72
		Y ask Y	4267.49
		Big Ten Inch	4211.17
	Adult Centrifugal	Bad to the Bone	2704.59
		United Flingdom	1355.14
		J.D. Lazarus	187.57
	Adult Catapult	Fibonacci Unlimited 2	2862.28
		Hypertension	2295.47
		Sir Chunks-a-Lot	1851.39
	Adult Trebuchet	Yankee Siege	1702.46
		PumpkinHammer	1260.66
		King Arthur	1098.04
	Adult Human Powered	Gene's Machine	1452.24
		Pumpkin Slayer	1423.72
		Destrier	1036.32
	Adult Torsion	Onager	1640.69
		Chucky II	1422.33
		Roman Revenge	1059.64
	Adult Centrifugal Human Powered	M2S2 Spinumpkin	229.59
		Spinning Wheel	220.39
		Pumpkin Putter	141.50
	Youth 11-17 Air Cannon	Redneck's Dream	3669.78
		Iron Tiger	3157.81
		Ozone Blaster	3052.62
	Youth 11-17 Catapult	Little Feats	1232.94
		Cross Your Fingers	590.11
		Tremors	552.63
	Youth 11-17 Trebuchet	Pumpkin Whipper	749.00
		Punkin Planter	623.76
		Monster Blaster	422.73
	Youth 11-17 Human Powered	Pavement Princess	397.88
		Crew 77	277.75
		Troop-u-chat	96.65
	Youth 10 & Under	Pomeroy Sister Slinger	465.17
		Iron Monger	349.04
		Little Liberty	221.74
	Theatrical	Pirates of Punkin Chunkin'	
		Punkin Trap	
		Lunch Launcher	

Year	Class	Team	Distance (feet)
2006**	Adult Air Cannon	2nd Amendment	3870.50
		Fire & Ice	3646.20
		Old Glory	3632.59
	Adult Centrifugal	Bad to the Bone	2737.69
		De-Terminator	1097.68
		J.D. Lazarus	935.17
	Adult Catapult	Fibonacci Unlimited II	2020.43
		Sir Chunks-A-Lot	1948.27
		Hypertension	1727.44
	Adult Trebuchet	Yankee Siege	1476.52
		King Arthur	1116.52
		Morgana	757.96
	Adult Human Powered	Gene's Machine	1466.82
		Pumpkin Slayer	1273.24
		Mischief Knights	1271.13
	Adult Torsion	Chucky II	2020.76
		Onager	1302.17
		Mista Ballista	670.18
	Youth Air Cannon	Ozone Blaster	3718.51
		Snot Rocket	2933.93
		Little Blasters	2653.11
	Youth Catapult	Tremors	794.62
		Punkin II	232.68
		Agent Orange	95.71
	Youth Trebuchet	Punkin Whipper	729.18
		Troop 6	589.62
		Yo'av Ben Tzruyah	531.27
	Youth Human Powered	Failed Negotiations	853.46
		Jack-O-Splatter	691.75
		Bob's Your Uncle	512.66
	Youth 10 & Under Catapult	Jersey Devil	248.54
		Little Liberty	218.45
	Youth 10 & Under Trebuchet	Sister Slinger	459.14
	Theatrical	Punkin Trap	
		Lunch Launcher	
		Pirates of the Punkin Chunk	
2007**	Adult Air Cannon	Big Ten Inch	4211.27
		Young Glory III	3579.62
		2nd Amendment	3552.72
	Adult Female Air Cannon	Let's Bounce	2932.36
		Dragon Lady	2879.48
		Bad Hair Day	2551.80

Year	Class	Team	Distance (feet)
2007 (continued)	Adult Centrifugal	Bad to the Bone	1852.88
		United Flingdom	1269.16
		De-Terminator	963.17
	Adult Catapult	Fibonacci Unlimited	2353.62
		Hypertension	1765.35
		Sir Chunks-A-Lot	1727.54
	Adult Trebuchet	Yankee Siege	1658.55
		Magic of Merlin	828.67
		PumpkinHammer	754.53
	Adult Human Powered	Gene's Machine	1816.29
		Mischief Knights	1596.54
		Pumpkin Slayer	1370.92
	Adult Torsion	Chucky	2152.93
		Roman Revenge II	2017.22
		Onager	1645.22
	Youth Air Cannon	Snot Rocket	3215.27
		Ozone Blaster	3028.75
		Little Blasters	2630.97
	Youth Human Powered	Rockville	583.22
		Bandit	373.86
	Youth Catapult	Little Feats	967.12
		Tremors	752.52
		Punkin Pitche	730.52
	Youth Trebuchet	Arbiter II	694.06
		Troop Six Shooter	584.94
		Got Her Did	544.26
	Youth 10 & Under Catapult	Pomeroy Sister Slinger	445.40
		Hatra Ballista	330.42
		Little Liberty	190.19
	Youth 10 & Under Trebuchet	Cucurbita Pepos Pitcher	447.84
		Jersey Devil	437.57
		Lontz Flingshot	327.53
	Theatrical	Punkin Trap	
		Lunch Launcher	

* Reports of the first year, including programs from subsequent events, contain various winning distances of 50 feet, 60 feet, 178 feet and 187 feet. But, Bill Thompson says the distance was 178 feet.

** Official World Championship Punkin Chunkin' Association records. Distances for other years are from various newspaper reports, from other chunkin' websites or chunkers' personal records. Some years are incomplete due to lack of records.

*** Technically, "Twin Aero" threw farther than "Mean Green Pumpkin Machine" with a toss of just over 460 feet, but it's not clear if it could truly be part of the competition. It was a biplane.

**** Won in a shoot-off.

RECORD YOUR OWN ANNUAL RESULTS

Year	Class	Team	Distance (feet)
	Adult Air Cannon	1st 2nd 3rd	
	Adult Female Air Cannon	1st 2nd 3rd	
	Adult Centrifugal	1st 2nd 3rd	
	Adult Catapult	1st 2nd 3rd	
	Catapult	1st 2nd 3rd	
	Adult Trebuchet	1st 2nd 3rd	
	Adult Human Powered	1st 2nd 3rd	
	Adult Torsion	1st 2nd 3rd	
	Youth Air Cannon	1st 2nd 3rd	
	Youth Human Powered	1st 2nd 3rd	
	Youth Catapult	1st 2nd 3rd	
	Youth Trebuchet	1st 2nd 3rd	
	Youth 10 & Under Catapult	1st 2nd 3rd	
	Youth 10 & Under Trebuchet	1st 2nd 3rd	
	Theatrical	1st 2nd 3rd	
	(space for new classes)	1st 2nd 3rd	

RECORD YOUR OWN ANNUAL RESULTS

Year	Class	Team		Distance (feet)
	Adult Air Cannon	1st 2nd 3rd		
	Adult Female Air Cannon	1st 2nd 3rd		
	Adult Centrifugal	1st 2nd 3rd		
	Adult Catapult	1st 2nd 3rd		
	Catapult	1st 2nd 3rd		
	Adult Trebuchet	1st 2nd 3rd		
	Adult Human Powered	1st 2nd 3rd		
	Adult Torsion	1st 2nd 3rd		
	Youth Air Cannon	1st 2nd 3rd		
	Youth Human Powered	1st 2nd 3rd		
	Youth Catapult	1st 2nd 3rd		
	Youth Trebuchet	1st 2nd 3rd		
	Youth 10 & Under Catapult	1st 2nd 3rd		
	Youth 10 & Under Trebuchet	1st 2nd 3rd		
	Theatrical	1st 2nd 3rd		
	(space for new classes)	1st 2nd 3rd		

RECORD YOUR OWN ANNUAL RESULTS

Year	Class	Team		Distance (feet)
	Adult Air Cannon	1st 2nd 3rd		
	Adult Female Air Cannon	1st 2nd 3rd		
	Adult Centrifugal	1st 2nd 3rd		
	Adult Catapult	1st 2nd 3rd		
	Catapult	1st 2nd 3rd		
	Adult Trebuchet	1st 2nd 3rd		
	Adult Human Powered	1st 2nd 3rd		
	Adult Torsion	1st 2nd 3rd		
	Youth Air Cannon	1st 2nd 3rd		
	Youth Human Powered	1st 2nd 3rd		
	Youth Catapult	1st 2nd 3rd		
	Youth Trebuchet	1st 2nd 3rd		
	Youth 10 & Under Catapult	1st 2nd 3rd		
	Youth 10 & Under Trebuchet	1st 2nd 3rd		
	Theatrical	1st 2nd 3rd		
	(space for new classes)	1st 2nd 3rd		

SPACE FOR AUTOGRAPHS
Have your favorite chunkin' teams autograph this page

BIBLIOGRAPHY

BOOKS

Margiotta, Franklin D., ed. *Brassey's Encyclopedia of Military History and Biography*. Washington, London: Brassey's, 1994.

NEWSLETTERS
AND OTHER PUBLICATIONS

Brown, William L., publisher/illustrator; Allen, Cindy, ed. *International Journal of Pumpkin Tossing*, Vol 1, No 1. Takoma Park MD: self-published, Oct. 1991.

Burgett, Marelen, ed. Heave, *The Official Publication of the International Hurling Society*. Forth Worth TX: self-published, Oct. 1994.

Carlow, Jacqueline.; DeSilvio, Danielle; Hayter, Alicia; Mendenhall, Meredith Punkin Chunkin, *Final Report, Submitted to Department of Mechanical Engineering, Villanova University*. Villanova PA: April 26, 2006. (http://www09.homepage.villanova.edu/merideth.mendenhall/Punkin.pdf)

Farnworth, Michael. *Innovative Steps in Trebuchet Evolution*. May 2005. (http://www.thehurl.org/tiki-download_file.php?fileId=66)

Gabriel, Richard A. and Metz, Karen S. *A Short History of War: The Evolution of Warfare and Weapons*. Carlisle Barracks PA: Strategic Studies Institute, U.S. Army War College, June 30, 1992. (http://www.au.af.mil/au/awc/awcgate/gabrmetz/gabr0000.htm)

Sussex Visitors Guide, Fall 1993. Seaford DE: Chesapeake Publishing Corp.

Yilmaz, Emin. *Winning the World Punkin Chunkin' Competition With a Student Design Project*. Department of Technology, University of Maryland Eastern Shore. Princess Anne MD: 1994. (http://facstaffwebs.umes.edu/eyilmaz/punase99.pdf)

NEWSPAPERS & MAGAZINES
Associated Press
"Should Delaware Buy Land for Punkin Chunkin' Contest?", Georgetown DE: Mar. 31, 2005.

Cape Gazette
"Lewes Chamber Busy Planning Punkin Chunkin' Activities Nov. 6," Lewes De: Aug. 27-Sept. 2, 1993.

"Cold, Rainy Weather Can't Deter Avid Punkin Chunkers," Lewes DE: Nov. 12, 1993.

"Punkin Chunkin' Talk Heats Up," Lewes DE: Oct. 29 – Nov. 4, 1993.

"Pumpkin Chunkers Gather Nov. 6," Lewes DE: Nov. 5, 1993.

"Late-breaking News on Punkin Chunkin'." Lewes DE: Nov. 5, 1993.

"Wow! 9th Annual Punkin Chunkin' is a Crowd-Pleasing Event," Lewes DE: Nov. 11-16, 1994.

"Punkin Chunkin," Lewes DE: Nov. 4-10, 1994.

"Lewes Chamber Plans for Large Punkin Chunkin' Crowd," Lewes DE: Oct. 7-13, 1994.

"Chunkers Unionize; Negotiate Series of Demands with event Organizers," Lewes DE: Oct. 7-13, 1994.

"Punkin Chunkin' Calls Flooding Lewes Chamber Offices; Volunteers Needed," Lewes DE: Oct. 28 – Nov. 3, 1994.

"Punkin Chunkin' Group Looks to New Sponsor," Lewes DE: Feb. 17, 1995.

"Punkin Chunkers Join Forces with Roadhouse to Expand Event." Lewes De: Mar. 3-9, 1995.

"Mello Yello's 2,655' Chunk Takes Punkin Championship," Lewes DE: Nov. 10-16, 1995.

"Chunkers Entertain Millions on CBS," Lewes DE: Nov. 3-9, 1995.

"It's 1995 and Thousands Watch Pumpkins Fly," Lewes DE: Nov. 10-16, 1995.

"Punkin Chunkin' to Splat Out Over Two Days North of Lewes," Lewes DE: Oct. 27-Nov. 2, 1995.

"Punkin Chunkers Prepare for Event Amidst Rumors of Giant Midwest Machine," Lewes DE: Oct. 25-31, 1996.

"Out-of-Towners Steal Punkin Chunkin' Title But Fans Depart With Memories of Chunk Full of Fun," Lewes DE: Nov. 8-14, 1996.

"Punkin Chunkin' Organizers Hope to Iron Out a Few Chinks," Lewes DE: Nov. 8-14, 1996.

"Punkin Chunkers Return From Illinois With a First Place," Lewes DE: Sept. 19-25, 1997

"Forget Falling Stocks, It's Punkin Chunkin' Time," Lewes DE: Oct. 31-Nov. 6, 1997.

"Chunkin' Fans Battle Muddy Ground to Watch Sussex Regain Crown," Lewes DE: Nov. 7-13, 1997.

"Punkin Chunkin' Must Move to a New Location," Lewes DE: Nov. 7-13, 1997.

"Punkin Chunkers, Roadhouse Split; Chunkers Plan to Keep Event in Sussex," Lewes DE: May 22-28, 1998.

"Punkin Chunkin' Energy Continuing to Build," Lewes DE: Oct. 23-29, 1998.

"Punkin Chunkin' World Championship Ready to Go at New Location," Lewes DE: Nov. 6-12, 1998.

"Melson Defaces Trophy, Literally, to Protest Loss of Pumpkin at Competition," Lewes DE: Nov. 20-26, 1998.

"Punkin Chunkers Gearing Up for 14th Annual Competition Nov. 6-7," Lewes DE: Oct. 15-21, 1999.

"Local Chunkers Do Well in Illinois and New York," Lewes DE: Oct. 22-28, 1999.

"On Eve of 14th World Championship Punkin Chunkin', Letterman Tries Again," Lewes DE: Nov. 5-11, 1999.

"Punkin Chunkers to Hurl Their Gourds For 15th Year Nov. 4-5," Lewes DE: Oct. 27-Nov. 2, 2000.

"Punkin Chunkin' Board of Directors Denies Appeal," Lewes DE: Nov. 17-23, 2000.

"Wolfman Aims Old Glory Toward New Record," Lewes DE: Nov. 2-9, 2001.

"Punkin Chunk Founders Honored at Ceremony," Lewes DE: Nov. 23-29, 2001.

"Gourds Fly in World Championship Punkin Chunkin'," Lewes DE: Nov. 8-14, 2002.

"Punkin Chunkin' Expands Classes for 2003 Competitions," Lewes DE: Oct. 24-30, 2003.

"State Expresses Concern Over Punkin Chunkin' Equipment Safety," Lewes DE: Nov. 21-27, 2003.

"Punkin Chunkin' to Have Last Shot at Hollyville Site," Lewes DE: July 30-Aug. 2, 2004.

"Punkin Chunkin' to Remain," Lewes DE: May 10-12, 2005.

"British Are Coming! UK Reality Show to Film Chunk," Lewes DE: Nov. 2-7, 2005.

"Punkin Chunkin' Continues to Support Local Charities," Lewes DE: Oct. 27-30, 2006.

"Punkin Chunkin' Bids Fond Farewell to Millsboro Field," Lewes DE: Nov. 10-13, 2006.

"Thompson Family Puts the 'Punkin in Punkin Chunkin'," Lewes DE: Nov. 6-8, 2007.

"Chunked Visitor Prepares for 2008," Lewes DE: Nov. 23-26, 2007.

Delaware Coast Press
"Pumpkins Chunked for New Record," Rehoboth Beach DE: Nov __, 1990.

"'90 Record Stands at '91 Punkin Chunkin'," Rehoboth Beach DE: Nov. 6, 1991.

"It's Time for Punkin Chunkin'," Rehoboth Beach DE: Nov. 4, 1992.

"The Punkins Were Flying High," Rehoboth Beach DE: Nov. 11, 1992.

"Chunkin' '93: Poetry in Commotion," Rehoboth Beach DE: Nov. 10, 1993.

"Punkin Chunkin'," Rehoboth Beach DE: Nov. 2, 1994.

"The Art of Chunkin'," Rehoboth Beach DE: Nov. 2, 1994.

"Airborne Pumpkins Abound for Festival," Rehoboth Beach DE: Nov. 3, 1993.

"Air Cannon Sets New World Record at Punkin Chunkin'," Rehoboth Beach DE: Nov. 9, 1994.

"Punkin Chunkin'," Rehoboth Beach DE: Nov. 1, 1995.

"'Mello Yello' Wins Punkin Chunkin'," Rehoboth Beach DE: Nov. 8, 1995.

"Have Gourd, Will Travel," Rehoboth Beach DE: Oct. 30, 1996

"Illinois Chunker Takes Home Trophy," Rehoboth Beach DE: Nov. 6, 1996.

"Lewes Team Regains Punkin Chunkin' Title," Rehoboth Beach DE: Nov. 5, 1997.

"Punkin Chunkin' 1998 Will Feature More Space, Less Circus Near Angola," Lewes DE: Nov. 10, 1998.

"Punkin Chunkin '98: A New Field, More Competition, Flaring Tempers," Lewes DE: Nov. 13-19, 1998.

Delaware State News
"It's a Bird... It's a plane... It's...," Dover DE: Nov. 8, 1987

"Thousands Turn Out for Pumpkin Chunkin'," Dover DE: Nov. 8, 1992.

"Punkin Chunkin' a Winner," Dover DE: June 18, 1993.

"Slingin' in the Rain," Dover DE: Nov. 7, 1993.

"Ready for Takeoff," Dover DE: Nov. 4, 1994

"Man Hurt During Chunkin' Set Up," Dover DE: Nov. 5, 1994.

"Chunkin' Enters a New Era," Dover DE: Nov. 6, 1994.

"Plumber 'Tinkers' Toward a Winning Tradition," Dover DE: Dec. 4, 1994.

"Punkin Chunkers Blame It on the Rain," Dover DE: Nov. 1, 1995.

New Hampshire Union Leader
"Operator of Pumpkin Tosser Injured in Freak Accident," Manchester NH: Sept. 24, 2007.

Philadelphia Inquirer
"How Far Will Pumpkins Fly? 178 Feet," Philadelphia PA: Nov. ___, 1986.

"Hurtling Pumpkins Catching On," Philadelphia PA: Dec. 11, 1994.

Southern Delaware Explorer
"World Championship Punkin Chunkin' Nov. 1-3," Vol. 7, No. 10. Ocean View DE: Nov. 2002

Southern Delaware Magazine
"Punkins Away," Rehoboth Beach DE: November 1992.

"Flying Pumpkins Bring Bragging Rights to Chunkers," Rehoboth Beach DE: October 1993.

Sports Illustrated
"Pumpkin, Two O'Clock High!," Dec. 12, 1994.

The Kennett Paper
"Science Wiz Tom Burns Leads Team to Punkin Chunkin' Glory," Kennett Square PA: Nov. 16, 2006.

The Michigan Daily
"Businessman Defends Hurling Record with Pumpkin Gun, " University of Michigan. Ann Arbor MI: Nov. 2, 2004.

The New York Times.
"An Actor Demoralized by Tomatoes," New York NY: Oct. 28, 1883.

The News Journal
"Pumpkin 'Chunkers' Eye Pie in the Sky," Wilmington DE: Nov. 4, 1990.

"Here, It's OK to be Out of Their Gourds," Wilmington DE: Nov. __, 1991.

"World-class Competition Squashes Chunkin' Records," Wilmington DE: Nov. 8, 1992.

"Jack Splat," Wilmington DE: Nov 5-7, 1993.

"Chunkin' Record No Flight of Fancy," Wilmington DE: Nov. 1, 1993.

"P(umpkin) Shooters," Wilmington DE: Nov. 4-6, 1994.

"Punkin Chunkin Contest in Lewes Has People Out of Their Gourds," Wilmington DE: Nov. 6, 1994.

"Pumpkins Rain Down on New York," Wilmington DE: Nov. 1, 1995.

"Extra Chunky," Wilmington DE: Nov. 3-5, 1995.

"Pumpkin Pitchers Go for the Gourd," Wilmington DE: Nov. 5, 1995.

"King of the Fling," Wilmington DE: Nov. 1-3, 1996.

"Out-of-Staters' Punkin Chunkin' Victory Stands," Wilmington DE: Nov. 5, 1996.

"Outchunked by Outsiders," Wilmington DE: Nov. 5, 1996.

"Men & Machines (and Fruit)," Wilmington DE: Oct. 31, 1997.

"Chunkers Aim to Catapult to Fame," Wilmington DE: Nov. 2, 1997.

"Chunkin' Title Returns," Wilmington DE: Nov. 3, 1997.

"Punkin Chunkin' Outgrows Its Patch," Wilmington DE: Nov. 1, 1997.

"Throws and Thrills by the Thousands," Wilmington DE: Nov. 7, 1998.

"Punkin Chunk Crown Hauled back to Illinois," Wilmington DE: Nov. 9, 1998.

"Punkin Chunkin' Goes International," Wilmington DE: Nov. 2, 2005.

"Annual Gourd-Hurling Contest Turned into Punkin Chunkin' for One 10-year-old," Wilmington DE: Nov. 20, 2007.

"A Final Resting Place at Sea," Wilmington DE: May 26, 2008.

The Wall Street Journal
"A Scud It's Not, But the Trebuchet Hurls a Mean Piano," New York NY: July 30, 1991

The Washington Post
"Gourd Vibrations," Washington DC: Nov. 1, 1992.

The Whale
"Pumpkins Fly Through Sussex Skies," Lewes DE: Nov. 11, 1987.

"Bombs away at Third Annual Pumpkin Chunk," Lewes DE: Nov. 9, 1988.

"Fourth Pumpkin Chunk Set Nov. 4 Near Lewes," Lewes DE: Oct. 21, 1989.

"Sussex Pumpkin Chunkin' High Flyin' Affair," Lewes DE: Nov. 8, 1989.

"Annual Pumpkin Chunk Set Nov. 3 Near Lewes," Lewes DE: Oct. 27, 1990.

"World Champion Punkin Chunkers Duel to Finish," Lewes DE: Nov. 7, 1990.

"Punkin Chunkin Battle Looms Saturday North of Lewes," Lewes DE: Oct. 30, 1991.

"Ultimate Warrior Carves Niche in Punkin Chunk History," Lewes DE: Nov. 6, 1991.

"Chunkers Feel Duped by Dave," Lewes DE: Nov. 2, 1995.

OTHER DOCUMENTS

Financial report 1992 and 1993 World Championship Punkin Chunkin'
Financial report 1997 and 1998 World Championship Punkin Chunkin'
Financial report 1999 World Championship Punkin Chunkin'
Financial report 2000 and 2001 World Championship Punkin Chunkin'
Form letter from Capt. Harry "Speed" Lackhove announcing toilet chunk. Lewes DE: December 1997.

Letter to Lewes Chamber of Commerce from Larry McLaughlin with demands from United Pumpkin Chunkers Local 69. Lewes DE: Sept. 24, 1994.

Letter to Larry McLaughlin from John Ellsworth with "Punkin Chunkin' Strike Form U812." Lewes DE: Sept. 27, 1994

Letter to John Ellsworth from Larry McLaughlin concerning Sept. 29, 1994 meeting to address grievances. Lewes DE: Oct. 6, 1994

List of donations from 1995 World Championship Punkin Chunkin'

Official and Safety Rules Handbook, World Championship Punkin Chunkin' Association, Rev. 8. Jan. 6, 2007.

Programs for annual event, 1991 through 1994, Lewes Chamber of Commerce.

Programs for annual event, 1995 through 1997, Roadhouse Steak Joint.

Roadhouse Steak Joint Proposal of Events and Rules for 1995 World Championship Punkin Chunkin'.

Response to list of "strike" demands. Lewes DE: Sept. 29, 1994.

INTERVIEWS

Brenneman, Margie. Telephone interview. June 6, 2008. Lewes DE.

Brewster, Terry. June 23, 2008. Georgetown DE.

Browne, Lana. April 23, 2008. Milton DE.

Burton, Charles. May 20, 2008. Milton DE.

Burton, Jake. May 20, 2008. Milton DE

Coulbourne, Stephanie. June 8, 2008. Milton DE.

Ellsworth, John. May 17, 2008. Lewes DE.

Hazzard, Michael. June 6, 2008. Lewes DE.

Lackhove, Harry. May 21, 2008. Lewes DE.

McLaughlin, Larry. April 22, 2008. Lewes DE.

Melson, Betty. June 23, 2008. Georgetown DE.

Nelson, Eric. June 23, 2008. Georgetown DE.

Nelson, Trish. June 23, 2008. Georgetown DE.

Pepper, Donald. May 3, 2008. Rehoboth DE.

Shade, Frank E. July 13, 2008. Nassau DE.

Sharp, William. May 20, 2008. Milton DE.

Thompson, William. April 24, 2008. Georgetown DE.

Zigman, Diane. June 6, 2008. Lewes DE.

WORLD WIDE WEB

Angelfire
http://www.angelfire.com/geek/CatapultChiks/ancientcatapults

American Profile.com
http://www.americanprofile.com/article/2685.html?printable=true

Answers.com
http://www.answers.com/topic/keg-tossing

BBC
http://www.bbc.co.uk/dna/h2g2/A973703

Big 10 Inch
http://www.geocities.com/zbig10inch/

Channel4.com
http://www.channel4.com/4car/ontv/scrapheap/challenges/16_punkin_chunk/

http://www.channel4.com/4car/ontv/scrapheap/challenges/16_punkin_chunk/result.html

CNNMoney.com
http://money.cnn.com/2002/08/15/pf/saving/travel/falldrives_pumpkins/index.htm

Chunker's, An Unofficial Website of Punkin Chunk Information
http://www.geocities.com/heartland/acres/8558/

Encyclopedia Britannica
Encyclopedia Britannica, 2008, Encyclopedia Britannica Online Library Edition, 22 Mar. 2008
http://library.eb.com

ESPN News
http://sports.espn.go.com/outdoors/general/news/story?id=3107378

Fibonacci
http://www.norwellma.com/pumpkin.htm

Google Answers, History of egg and tomato throwing as a form of protest
http://answers.google.com/answers/threadview?id=217280

Iowa State Daily.com
http://media.www.iowastatedaily.com/media/storage/paper818/news/1998/11/12/UndefinedSection/Isu-Ready.For.Chuckin.Pumpkins-1073318.shtml

Loaded Boing
http://www.geocities.com/Pipeline/Curb/5460/index.html

Medieval castle siege weapons.com
http://www.medieval-castle-siege-weapons.com/ballista.html

http://www.medieval-castle-siege-weapons.com/ballista-catapults.html

http://www.medieval-castle-siege-weapons.com/ballista-plans.html

http://www.medieval-castle-siege-weapons.com/history-of-trebuchets.html

http://www.medieval-castle-siege-weapons.com/onager-catapult.html

http://www.medieval-castle-siege-weapons.com/tension-catapults.html

http://www.medieval-castle-siege-weapons.com/trebuchet-history.html

Middle Ages.org
http://www.middle-ages.org.uk/ballista.htm

http://www.middle-ages.org.uk/catapults.htm

http://www.middle-ages.org.uk/trebuchet.htm

Midrealm.org
http://www.midrealm.org/mkyouth/links/catapults.htm

Morton Chamber of Commerce
http://www.pumpkincapital.com/index.php?section=7

NJ Hurl
http://www.njhurl.com

NPR, Morning Edition
http://www.npr.org/templates/story/story.php?storyId=5007873

Onager Online
http://www.onager.net/

PumpkinHammer
http://www.bidlink.com/pumpkinhammer/index.htm

Punkin Chuckin' in the Pumpkin Capital
http://www.douglascoulter.com/Personal/body_punkin__chuckin_.html

RoadsideAmerica.com
http://www.roadsideamerica.com/tips/getAttraction.php?tip_AttractionNo==2188

http://www.roadsideamerica.com/news/16729

Second Amendment
  http://www.secondamendmentgun.us/

Slinging.org
  http://slinging.org/4.html

Spanish Fiestas
  http://www.spanish-fiestas.com/spanish-festivals/
  la-tomatina-tomato-battle-bunyol.htm

The Free-Lance Star
  http://www.fredericksburg.com/News/
  FLS/2005/102005/10242005/139732

The Big 10 Inch
  http://www.geocities.com/zbig10inch/

The Grey Company
  http://members.iinet.net.au/~bill/greyco.html

Tomato Casual
  http://www.tomatocasual.com/2008/02/07/the-
  history-of-throwing-rotten-tomatoes/

Tour Egypt
  http://www.touregypt.net/featurestories/games.
  htm

Wikipedia

  http://en.wikipedia.org/wiki/Ballista

  http://en.wikipedia.org/wiki/Catapult

  http://en.wikipedia.org/wiki/Highland_games

  http://en.wikipedia.org/wiki/Olympics

  http://en.wikipedia.org/wiki/Sling_%28weapon%29

  http://en.wikipedia.org/wiki/Slingshot

  http://en.wikipedia.org/wiki/Vespasian

World Championship Punkin Chunkin' Association

  http://www.punkinchunkin.com/

COLOPHON

Pie in the Sky: the Authorized History of Punkin Chunkin' was composed with a family of serif and sans serif faces, Arno and Gill Sans.

The text was set in 12 point Arno Pro regular with 2 point leading. Gill Sans was used for the book's front and back material, text, titles and captions.

The book was designed in Italy by Bob Schwartz of FotoGrafics using Adobe InDesign on an Apple Macintosh computer.

It was printed and bound in the United States of America on 50 pound book with a 10 point coated cover, laminated for durability.

Arno, a recent addition to the Adobe font catalog, was designed by Adobe's principal designer, Robert Slimbach and named after the river that runs through the capital of Renaissance Italy, Florence. Though heavily influenced by the warmth and readability of early humanist typefaces of the 15th and 16th centuries, Arno is clearly a contemporary typeface.

Gill Sans, a humanist sans serif, was designed by Eric Gill and released by the Monotype Corporation in the late 1920's. Though based on a 1916 typeface designed by British typographer Edward Johnson for the signage of the London Undeground, Gill's version is more classical in proportion.